Contents

Contents

Name ___________________________________

Weekly Lesson Test
Lesson 1

Selection Comprehension

Choose the best answer for each question.

1. How do you know "The Hot and Cold Summer" is realistic fiction?
   - Ⓐ It has facts and information about a subject.
   - Ⓑ The characters face problems that could happen in real life.
   - Ⓒ It explains why one person is important in history.
   - Ⓓ The story could not happen in real life.

2. Why does Bolivia suggest ordering a second pizza?
   - Ⓕ She wants the boys to realize they are just showing off.
   - Ⓖ She knows that Edna would rather have pizza than eggs.
   - Ⓗ She thinks that Mr. Dunn might like some.
   - Ⓘ She wants to eat a whole pizza by herself.

3. Which action BEST shows that Bolivia thinks Rory is a good friend?
   - Ⓐ She offers him some of her salad.
   - Ⓑ She agrees to eat part of his pizza.
   - Ⓒ She trusts him with the lemonade money.
   - Ⓓ She wants to get another pizza to eat.

4. What is the author's MAIN reason for writing "The Hot and Cold Summer"?
   - Ⓕ to show readers how to settle an argument
   - Ⓖ to let readers know that contests can be fun
   - Ⓗ to tell readers why pizza is a good food to eat
   - Ⓘ to show readers that friendship takes many forms

5. Why does Bolivia say that Rory is cheating?
   - Ⓐ He did not make the money selling lemonade.
   - Ⓑ He is not eating every part of the pizza.
   - Ⓒ He is able to eat only five slices of pizza.
   - Ⓓ He does not tell his mom about the contest.

Name ____________________

Weekly Lesson Test
Lesson 1

6. Why is Rory worried that he and Derek are no longer friends?
   Ⓕ because Rory has been riding bikes with Bolivia
   Ⓖ because Rory broke his word not to speak to Bolivia
   Ⓗ because Derek did not write Rory often from camp
   Ⓘ because Derek is upset Rory let Bolivia's parrot escape

7. What is the MOST LIKELY reason that Derek does not want to go swimming?
   Ⓐ He does not want to leave Rory alone.
   Ⓑ He would rather practice his card tricks.
   Ⓒ He wants to spend time selling lemonade.
   Ⓓ He does not really enjoy being in the water.

8. If the story "The Hot and Cold Summer" needed a new title, which would be BEST?
   Ⓕ Derek Makes a New Friend at Camp
   Ⓖ Lucette's Great Escape: A Bird's Tale
   Ⓗ The Mystery of the Missing Coin Purse
   Ⓘ Three Friends and a Great Pizza Challenge

Written Response

9. How do Rory's feelings change in the story? Use details from "The Hot and Cold Summer" to support your answer.

____

____

____

____

TOTAL SCORE: ______ /8 + ______ /2

Name ________________________________

Weekly Lesson Test
Lesson 1

Focus Skill: Character's Traits and Motivations

Read the passage. Then choose the best answer for each question.

The Gift

Last summer, Kayla visited her Aunt Mina for an entire week. They saw the sights of New York and ate in the park. But the best part was the two days that they spent at Kayla's favorite museum, the Museum of Modern Art.

At the museum, Kayla asked Aunt Mina whether she could visit the gift shop. She wanted a gift for Aunt Mina, a memento of their time together. She looked at posters, cards, and books and thought they were all beautiful. She knew her aunt would love a brightly colored poster. Kayla looked at the pricetags of some of the posters. She could never afford to spend so much! She wanted to give her aunt a gift, but she didn't have enough money. She left the gift shop very disappointed.

Later, as they walked to Aunt Mina's apartment, Aunt Mina noticed Kayla's sadness. When she asked Kayla what was wrong, Kayla told her about what had happened in the gift shop.

"Little One," she said, "Do not worry. Spending time with you is the only gift I need."

Kayla felt the same way about her aunt, but she still wanted to give her aunt a gift.

The next morning, Kayla stayed with Mrs. Gomez, Aunt Mina's neighbor. Aunt Mina had to run an errand. Kayla noticed a toolbox full of paints in the corner.

"Mrs. Gomez, I didn't know you were a painter," Kayla said.

"I paint a little," Mrs. Gomez said with a smile. "Your aunt tells me you love the art museum. Would you like to try to make a little art of your own?"

"I've never tried painting," Kayla said nervously. "I've only ever drawn."

Name ______________________

Weekly Lesson Test
Lesson 1

Kayla thought about the beautiful, vividly colored paintings at the museum. Then she had an idea.

"I could make a painting for Aunt Mina," she said. "It would be the perfect gift!"

---

1. What can you tell about Kayla from what she does and says?
   Ⓐ She is a thoughtful person.
   Ⓑ She thinks only of herself.
   Ⓒ She likes to learn new skills.
   Ⓓ She is afraid to try new things.

2. What can you tell about Aunt Mina from what she does and says?
   Ⓕ She is an talented artist.
   Ⓖ She enjoys taking walks.
   Ⓗ She is interested in art.
   Ⓘ She cares about her niece.

3. Why does Kayla decide to paint a picture?
   Ⓐ She wants to learn to be an artist.
   Ⓑ She wants to make her aunt a gift.
   Ⓒ She wants to make herself a poster.
   Ⓓ She wants to make Mrs. Gomez happy.

4. Which word best describes Kayla at the end of the passage?
   Ⓕ excited
   Ⓖ upset
   Ⓗ funny
   Ⓘ worried

Name ______________________________

Weekly
Lesson Test
Lesson 1

Synonyms and Antonyms

Choose the best answer for each question.

1. Read this sentence.

Roller-coaster rides thrilled Destiny.

What is a synonym for the word *thrilled*?

Ⓐ bored
Ⓑ scared
Ⓒ excited
Ⓓ worried

2. Read this sentence.

The teams played the final game of the competition yesterday.

What is a synonym for the word *competition*?

Ⓕ trial
Ⓖ dispute
Ⓗ agreement
Ⓘ contest

3. Read this sentence.

Maggie was certain that she would win.

What is an antonym for the word *certain*?

Ⓐ unsure
Ⓑ ungrateful
Ⓒ unashamed
Ⓓ uneasy

Name ___________________________________

Weekly
Lesson Test
Lesson 1

4. Read this sentence.

The new superstore at the mall is humongous.

What is an antonym for the word *humongous*?

Ⓕ beautiful
Ⓖ tiny
Ⓗ narrow
Ⓘ unusual

5. Read this sentence.

Your grades will improve if you study.

What is an antonym for the word *improve*?

Ⓐ change
Ⓑ increase
Ⓒ divide
Ⓓ worsen

TOTAL SCORE: ______ /5

Name ______________________________

Weekly Lesson Test
Lesson 1

Robust Vocabulary

Choose the word that best completes each sentence.

1. The group made a _____ to cooperate on the project.

Ⓐ pact
Ⓑ queasy
Ⓒ venture
Ⓓ depriving

2. I felt _____ on the boat and sat down to calm my stomach.

Ⓕ annoyed
Ⓖ queasy
Ⓗ curious
Ⓘ foisted

3. The coach _____ ten more sit-ups on us when we thought we were finished.

Ⓐ foisted
Ⓑ ventured
Ⓒ annoyed
Ⓓ needed

4. My idea of a successful business _____ would be owning a pizza restaurant.

Ⓕ office
Ⓖ pact
Ⓗ venture
Ⓘ meeting

Name ______________________________

Weekly Lesson Test
Lesson 1

5. Jamal _____ his older brother by singing off-key during the ride home.
   Ⓐ improved
   Ⓑ deprived
   Ⓒ foisted
   Ⓓ annoyed

6. Are you _____ your plants of water while you are away, or is someone caring for them?
   Ⓕ foisting
   Ⓖ traveling
   Ⓗ depriving
   Ⓘ providing

TOTAL SCORE: _____ /6

Name ______________________________

Weekly
Lesson Test
Lesson 1

Grammar: Declarative and Interrogative Sentences

Choose the best answer for each question.

1. Which sentence is a declarative sentence?

Ⓐ Anthony was at the park yesterday.
Ⓑ Anthony was at the park yesterday?
Ⓒ Anthony at the park yesterday.
Ⓓ Why was Anthony at the park yesterday.

2. Which sentence is a declarative sentence?

Ⓕ Are all of the players on the field?
Ⓖ The movie always starts on time.
Ⓗ Drove to school in the carpool today.
Ⓘ Because my favorite show was on.

3. Which sentence is an interrogative sentence?

Ⓐ I know that I can do better.
Ⓑ I can do better than that.
Ⓒ I think that I do better?
Ⓓ Why do you think I want to do better?

4. Which sentence is an interrogative sentence?

Ⓕ Tamara is coming to the festival.
Ⓖ At night when you are sleeping?
Ⓗ Is she going to call you tomorrow?
Ⓘ When my brother finishes his swim lesson.

TOTAL SCORE: ______ /4

Name ______________________________

Weekly
Lesson Test
Lesson 1

Oral Reading Fluency

Last Monday was Labor Day, my favorite holiday. My brother and I had the day off from school. Meanwhile, my mother and father did not have to go to work.

In the United States, most workers receive the day off on Labor Day. It is a special day to honor the hard work that Americans do. My mother says that Labor Day became an official holiday in 1894. Before that time, workers were not always treated well. They had to work long hours and they did not get adequate wages. Today, workers have shorter workdays and most people are paid a fair wage. Also, children are not permitted to work until they are old enough.

To celebrate Labor Day, my family has an annual picnic. This year we had our biggest celebration yet. Everyone we knew attended. In addition to my whole family being there, our neighbors and my school friends came. We played games, ate delicious food, and took time to relax. That night, my dad projected a movie on the side of our house while we sat on blankets on the grass and watched.

Our Labor Day picnic is my favorite celebration. It is the perfect way to relax with friends and to just take a break from the busy world. I can't wait until next Labor Day.

______ /WCPM

Name ______________________________

Weekly Lesson Test
Lesson 2

Selection Comprehension

Choose the best answer for each question.

1. At the beginning of the story, what is the MAIN reason the crowd is curious about Jackie?
   Ⓐ She plays for the Lookouts.
   Ⓑ She is small and delicate.
   Ⓒ She is a girl pitcher.
   Ⓓ She is very young.

2. How does the reader know that this story is biographical?
   Ⓕ Events are told in the order they happened.
   Ⓖ The characters do not behave like real people.
   Ⓗ The author tells about her own thoughts and feelings.
   Ⓘ The author tells the true story of a real person's life.

3. What is Jackie's main problem in the story?
   Ⓐ She wants to prove that she can pitch in the major leagues.
   Ⓑ She hopes to get more people to attend baseball games.
   Ⓒ She wants to switch from one baseball team to another.
   Ⓓ She wants to show that she is stronger than Babe Ruth.

4. With which statement would the author MOST LIKELY agree?
   Ⓕ To get ahead, it is important to know the right people.
   Ⓖ Determination and hard work can lead to success.
   Ⓗ People with natural talent do not require training.
   Ⓘ A wise person does not set goals too high.

5. Why does Babe Ruth think that women should not play baseball?
   Ⓐ They lack speed.
   Ⓑ They are not tough enough.
   Ⓒ They cannot aim well.
   Ⓓ They do not like to compete.

Name ______________________________

Weekly Lesson Test
Lesson 2

6. What happens RIGHT AFTER the umpire calls the first strike on Babe Ruth?
   Ⓕ Babe Ruth tips his cap at Jackie.
   Ⓖ Babe Ruth throws his bat on the ground.
   Ⓗ Jackie gets nervous and makes a mistake.
   Ⓘ Jackie pitches the ball to Lou Gehrig.

7. What BEST shows that Jackie has prepared for this contest?
   Ⓐ She practices pitching every day.
   Ⓑ She can bat as well as she can throw.
   Ⓒ She knows that the Yankees are a famous team.
   Ⓓ She knows what kind of pitch each batter expects.

8. Why is Jackie happy at the end of the story?
   Ⓕ She has proved her skill by striking out two of the best players.
   Ⓖ The game is over, and her team has the winning score.
   Ⓗ She thinks she will soon play on a major-league team.
   Ⓘ The crowd is cheering and clapping for her.

Written Response

9. **COMPARING TEXTS** How are Jackie in "Mighty Jackie: The Strike-Out Queen" and the new kid in "The New Kid" ALIKE and how are they DIFFERENT? Use information and details from the story AND the poem to explain your answer.

____

____

____

____

____

TOTAL SCORE: ______ /8 + ______ /2

Name ____________________

Weekly Lesson Test
Lesson 2

Focus Skill: Character's Traits and Motivations

Read the passage. Then choose the best answer for each question.

A Pet for Rico

Rico loved animals. He dreamed about becoming an animal doctor. Then he could be around animals all day and help them.

Although he liked tigers and hippos and parrots, cats and dogs were his favorites. Like many other children, Rico had always wanted a pet. When he went to his friends' houses, he helped feed their pets. He never minded taking the pets on walks or helping out with baths. Often when his friends' pets needed medicine, Rico was able to get the pill in the pet's mouth and make sure the pill was swallowed. He even was able to put drops in his friend's cat's eyes.

Rico felt ready to have his own pet, but his parents weren't sure. They thought he was too young to care for a pet. He needed to be responsible.

His mother said, "It's one thing to help your friends, but it's another to do it all the time by yourself. Caring for a pet can become a chore, and people often get tired of chores."

"Not me," Rico thought. To show his parents, Rico began acting responsibly at home. He did his chores without being reminded and without complaining. He studied hard and got good grades.

After a while, he asked his parents, "May I have a pet?"

They thought about it. Maybe Rico was ready after all. They certainly had noticed how Rico did his chores. They were proud of his schoolwork and his way with animals.

"What are you doing on Saturday?" Rico's father asked him. "Do you want to come to the mall with Mom and me?"

"The mall?" Rico moaned. "I don't like shopping."

"I think you could spare some time," his father said, smiling. "It's Pet Adoption Day at the mall."

Name ____________________

Weekly Lesson Test
Lesson 2

1. Which of these traits best describes Rico?
   Ⓐ lazy
   Ⓑ honest
   Ⓒ funny
   Ⓓ dependable

2. According to the passage, what motivates Rico to want to be an animal doctor?
   Ⓕ He wants to take care of animals.
   Ⓖ His mother is an animal doctor.
   Ⓗ He wants to train dogs and cats.
   Ⓘ His friends want to be animal doctors.

3. What does Rico's behavior toward animals show about him?
   Ⓐ He likes to play with others' pets.
   Ⓑ He is good at caring for animals.
   Ⓒ He would rather walk a dog than study.
   Ⓓ He thinks caring for animals is a chore.

4. How do Rico's parents' actions show that they are careful people?
   Ⓕ They believe that animals should not be house pets.
   Ⓖ They help their friends take care of their pets.
   Ⓗ They wait until Rico is responsible enough to have a pet.
   Ⓘ They want Rico to study to become an animal doctor.

TOTAL SCORE: ______ /4

Name ______________________________

Weekly
Lesson Test
Lesson 2

Synonyms and Antonyms

Choose the best answer for each question.

1. Read this sentence.

   All soldiers remained stationary until told to move.

   What is a synonym for *stationary*?

   Ⓐ quiet
   Ⓑ curious
   Ⓒ motionless
   Ⓓ nervous

2. Read this sentence.

   The teacher will demonstrate how to solve the problem.

   What is a synonym for *demonstrate*?

   Ⓕ write
   Ⓖ think
   Ⓗ ask
   Ⓘ show

3. Read this sentence.

   I tried to arrange the books in alphabetical order.

   What is an synonym for *arrange*?

   Ⓐ organize
   Ⓑ break
   Ⓒ measure
   Ⓓ open

Name ______________________________

Weekly
Lesson Test

Lesson 2

4. Read this sentence.

Water is a liquid.

What is an antonym for *liquid*?

Ⓕ mixture

Ⓖ solid

Ⓗ drink

Ⓘ paste

5. Read this sentence.

After her failure to reach the top of the mountain, the climber tried again.

What is an antonym for *failure*?

Ⓐ try

Ⓑ climb

Ⓒ success

Ⓓ discovery

TOTAL SCORE: ______ /5

Name ______________________________

Weekly Lesson Test
Lesson 2

Robust Vocabulary

▶ **Choose the word that best completes each sentence.**

1. His brave actions were _____, or famous, in the city of San Antonio.

Ⓐ muttered
Ⓑ legendary
Ⓒ queasy
Ⓓ depriving

2. Winning the lottery was a complete _____; such luck rarely strikes.

Ⓕ venture
Ⓖ pact
Ⓗ fluke
Ⓘ glare

3. She was surprised, and her mouth _____ wide open.

Ⓐ gaped
Ⓑ stunned
Ⓒ glared
Ⓓ muttered

4. My brother _____ when the bee stung him.

Ⓕ foisted
Ⓖ stunned
Ⓗ flinched
Ⓘ muttered

Name ______________________________

Weekly Lesson Test

Lesson 2

5. When I tripped, I heard some kids _____ at me.
   (A) depriving
   (B) foisting
   (C) glaring
   (D) snickering

6. I _____ at them, looking steadily until they stopped.
   (F) glared
   (G) gaped
   (H) stunned
   (I) annoyed

7. The surprise _____ Marco so much that he could not stand up.
   (A) flinched
   (B) foisted
   (C) stunned
   (D) muttered

8. Afraid to speak loudly, Rhonda _____ the answer under her breath.
   (F) glared
   (G) muttered
   (H) flinched
   (I) gaped

TOTAL SCORE: _____ /8

Name ___________________________________

Weekly Lesson Test
Lesson 2

Grammar: Imperative and Exclamatory Sentences and Interjections

▶ **Choose the best answer for each question.**

1. Which of the following is an imperative sentence?
Ⓐ The party was fun.
Ⓑ Have fun at the party.
Ⓒ Did you have fun at the party?
Ⓓ We had so much fun at the party!

2. Which of the following is an exclamatory sentence?
Ⓕ What a silly thing Jake did!
Ⓖ Jake did something silly.
Ⓗ Can you believe Jake did that?
Ⓘ Stop doing silly things, Jake.

3. Which of the following is an imperative sentence?
Ⓐ Arturo and Talia play soccer.
Ⓑ Whose team will you play on?
Ⓒ Practice kicking into the net first.
Ⓓ They had such a great time playing soccer!

4. Which of the following sentences contains an interjection?
Ⓕ Yikes! There's a mouse under the chair!
Ⓖ Please move your chair.
Ⓗ Did you see the mouse under the chair?
Ⓘ I've never seen a mouse before.

TOTAL SCORE: _____ /4

Name ______________________________

Weekly Lesson Test
Lesson 2

Oral Reading Fluency

The United States flag has not always looked as it does today. Over the years, it has gone through a number of variations. The first official flag, made in 1777, was entitled the "Stars and Stripes." It used stars and stripes as symbols for the earliest states.

At that time, the government had no regulations about the size of the flag. Therefore, some early flags were big, while others were small. On some flags the arrangement of the stars was in a circle, but in others the stars appeared in rows.

However, Congress would eventually make rules about the United States flag. Congress decided that the stars should appear in rows. Congress also made rules about the flag's size and shape. Even the colors were given official meanings. White is for purity, red is bravery, and blue is justice.

As a new state joined the union, the flag would receive a star and a stripe. In 1818, members of Congress changed that rule. They said that the flag would always have thirteen stripes to remind Americans of the first thirteen states. Only the number of stars would change. In 1960, the last star was added for Hawaii, the last state to join the union. The United States has fifty states, so now its flag has fifty stars.

The stars show how the United States has grown. The stripes remind us where our nation started. Did you know that our flag had so much meaning?

_______ /WCPM

Name ______________________________

Weekly Lesson Test
Lesson 3

Selection Comprehension

Choose the best answer for each question.

1. At the beginning of the poem, what is the MAIN reason Danitra suggests the summer activities?
   - Ⓐ She knows Zuri cannot think of things to do on her own.
   - Ⓑ She is bragging to Zuri about all the fun she plans to have.
   - Ⓒ She is showing Zuri there is a lot she can do during vacation.
   - Ⓓ She wants to know exactly what Zuri is doing while she is away.

2. How does Zuri feel when Danitra wants Zuri to see her off at the station?
   - Ⓕ angry
   - Ⓖ fearful
   - Ⓗ excited
   - Ⓘ relieved

3. Why does Danitra compare the night sky to an overcoat?
   - Ⓐ because both are big
   - Ⓑ because both are comforting
   - Ⓒ because both are thick and heavy
   - Ⓓ because both are dark

4. Why does Danitra think Zuri might like being in the country?
   - Ⓕ She would be able to learn to plow.
   - Ⓖ She could watch different insects.
   - Ⓗ She would have many more friends.
   - Ⓘ She would enjoy swimming in the lake.

5. How can readers tell this is a narrative poem?
   - Ⓐ It exaggerates the strength of a hero.
   - Ⓑ It tells a story.
   - Ⓒ It has events that could not really happen.
   - Ⓓ It has characters that try to solve a mystery.

Name ______________________________

Weekly Lesson Test
Lesson 3

6. What is this poem mostly about?
   Ⓕ how summers in the city are fun
   Ⓖ what it is like to visit the country
   Ⓗ how two friends enjoy a summer apart
   Ⓘ why the Fourth of July is an important holiday

7. Why does Danitra refuse to jump down from the tree she climbs?
   Ⓐ She is afraid of high places.
   Ⓑ She does not like the tough kids.
   Ⓒ She does not do anything she is dared to do.
   Ⓓ She is too smart to do something dangerous.

8. How does the reader know that Zuri is jealous of Danitra's trip?
   Ⓕ She thinks about trips she wishes she could take.
   Ⓖ She tries to make a new friend while Danitra is gone.
   Ⓗ She does not want to follow any of Danitra's big plans.
   Ⓘ She does not want to talk to Danitra when she gets home.

Written Response

9. Compare the way Danitra and Zuri celebrate the Fourth of July. How are their celebrations ALIKE and how are they DIFFERENT? Use information and details from the story to explain your answer.

____

____

____

____

TOTAL SCORE: ______ /8 + ______ /2

Name ____

Weekly Lesson Test
Lesson 3

Focus Skill: Compare and Contrast

▶ **Read the passage. Then choose the best answer for each question.**

Soccer and Softball

Amelia is trying to decide whether to play soccer or softball in the after-school sports league. Her friends are joining teams, and Amelia likes the idea that both soccer and softball are team sports. She also likes the fact that soccer and softball are outdoor sports. Her parents think that she spends too much time indoors. Both sports have referees, too. The referee judges the plays and decides whether the players have obeyed the rules. Both sports have coaches. Amelia would like to learn from a coach who could help her become a better player.

Of course, the sports are different, too. In soccer, players kick a large, soft ball. In softball, players use a bat to hit a small, hard ball, although it is "softer" than a baseball. The soccer field is all grass. The softball field has grass in the outfield and a combination of dirt and grass in the infield. In soccer, only the goalie can catch the ball. No one else can touch it with his or her hands. In softball, any fielder can catch the ball, and there is no kicking. In soccer, the players do a lot of running. In softball, the batter runs to a base, and the fielders run when they make a play.

Amelia likes both sports. She thinks that she'll get more exercise from playing soccer, but she likes to throw and catch. What will she decide to do?

Name ______________________________

Weekly Lesson Test
Lesson 3

1. What is being compared in this passage?
   Ⓐ leagues
   Ⓑ friends
   Ⓒ sports
   Ⓓ referees

2. What do soccer and softball have in common?
   Ⓕ the size of the ball
   Ⓖ the composition of the field
   Ⓗ the presence of a coach
   Ⓘ the use of a bat

3. How are soccer and softball different?
   Ⓐ Only softball has a goalie who can catch.
   Ⓑ Only softball is played outside.
   Ⓒ Only a soccer field has grass and dirt.
   Ⓓ Only soccer allows kicking the ball.

4. What does Amelia like about both soccer and softball?
   Ⓕ Both offer the same amount of exercise.
   Ⓖ Both are outdoor team sports.
   Ⓗ Her parents suggested the sports.
   Ⓘ Both have the same number of rules.

TOTAL SCORE: ______ /4

Name ______________________________

Weekly Lesson Test
Lesson 3

Robust Vocabulary

▶ **Choose the word that best completes each sentence.**

1. When the food ______ on the grill, you know it is hot.

Ⓐ strolls
Ⓑ clusters
Ⓒ sizzles
Ⓓ surrenders

2. She is very ______ about her choices; no other fruit is acceptable.

Ⓕ particular
Ⓖ queasy
Ⓗ legendary
Ⓘ stunned

3. The stars were ______ brightly last night in the sky.

Ⓐ sizzling
Ⓑ snickering
Ⓒ flinching
Ⓓ sparkling

4. Will you ______ along the path or run fast?

Ⓕ sparkle
Ⓖ stroll
Ⓗ venture
Ⓘ sizzle

Name ______________________________

Weekly
Lesson Test
Lesson 3

5. Giving up, Max said, "I _____."

Ⓐ stroll

Ⓑ glare

Ⓒ surrender

Ⓓ mutter

6. Did the flowers come in _____ or separately?

Ⓕ flukes

Ⓖ glares

Ⓗ snickers

Ⓘ clusters

TOTAL SCORE: _____ /6

Name ___________________________________

Weekly
Lesson Test
Lesson 3

Grammar: Subjects and Predicates

Choose the best answer for each question.

1. What is the subject of this sentence?

   Luisa and Travis were watching the rain pour down.

   Ⓐ Lucia and Travis
   Ⓑ were watching
   Ⓒ the rain
   Ⓓ pour down

2. What is the predicate in this sentence?

   After dinner, my older cousins went out.

   Ⓕ After dinner
   Ⓖ my older
   Ⓗ cousins
   Ⓘ went out

3. Which of these is missing its subject?

   Ⓐ My shampoo is missing.
   Ⓑ Turned the other way.
   Ⓒ On Sunday, Madison.
   Ⓓ The bears and the lions.

4. Which of these is missing its predicate?

   Ⓕ The tub has a leak.
   Ⓖ This summer the dog.
   Ⓗ Will not go without her.
   Ⓘ The wind blew, and the kite rose.

TOTAL SCORE: ______ /4

Name ______________________________

Weekly
Lesson Test
Lesson 3

Oral Reading Fluency

Manny is a yellow Labrador retriever who lives next door with Mrs. Brown, my neighbor. Manny has the peculiar habit of eating peoples' gloves. Manny sometimes gets in trouble when he misbehaves, but then he always ends up making friends with his gloveless victims.

Once, on a walk, Manny pulled a mitten off a little boy's hand while his mother and Mrs. Brown stood talking. That might have made someone angry or scared, but Manny is so gentle that no one knew it happened until the women finished talking. The boy's mother asked him where his mitten was. Manny tried to look innocent, but then Mrs. Brown saw a red thread hanging from Manny's chin. Rather than get upset, the boy and his mother just giggled and scratched Manny's head.

This summer Mrs. Brown visited her family in the country, where Manny's glove activities reached a new peak. Since it was the country, Manny was able to run loose and visit neighbors in their gardens. On his first trip, Manny returned with a pair of purple-striped garden gloves. On later trips he came back with even more gloves. When Mrs. Brown discovered Manny's clever plot, she went to each of the neighbors and offered to pay for the gloves. The neighbors just laughed and thanked her and said not to worry. They had enjoyed chasing Manny.

_______ /WCPM

Name ____________________

Weekly Lesson Test
Lesson 4

Selection Comprehension

Choose the best answer for each question.

1. Which reason BEST tells why the author wrote this story?
   - Ⓐ to describe an ocean trip from China to the United States
   - Ⓑ to describe the experience of immigrants from China
   - Ⓒ to show what the guards on Angel Island were like
   - Ⓓ to explain what life was once like in San Francisco

2. What is Kai's main problem in the story?
   - Ⓕ He misses his mother's special porridge.
   - Ⓖ He does not know how to play basketball.
   - Ⓗ He is afraid he will not be allowed to go to his father.
   - Ⓘ He cannot sleep in the new place because of the noise.

3. How do Kai and Young spend most of the first morning on the island?
   - Ⓐ eating bowls of watery rice
   - Ⓑ watching a basketball game
   - Ⓒ playing mah jong
   - Ⓓ standing in line

4. Why does the author compare some men on the island to "caged tigers"?
   - Ⓕ because both feel trapped and angry
   - Ⓖ because both are strong
   - Ⓗ because both can move quickly
   - Ⓘ because both are fierce and hungry

5. What did Kai dislike MOST about living on the island?
   - Ⓐ noisy people
   - Ⓑ scratchy opera
   - Ⓒ endless waiting
   - Ⓓ early bedtime

Name ______________________________

Weekly Lesson Test
Lesson 4

6. Why does the man in the bunk below Kai's write on the wall?
   Ⓕ He wants to be a writer.
   Ⓖ He wants to go home.
   Ⓗ He misses the outdoors.
   Ⓘ He wants to express his feelings.

7. How do you know that "Kai's Journey to Gold Mountain" is historical fiction?
   Ⓐ It tells a story that is set in a real place in the past.
   Ⓑ It gives facts about a topic.
   Ⓒ It has stage directions and is divided into scenes.
   Ⓓ It is written to teach a lesson.

8. When Kai leaves, why doesn't Young look at him?
   Ⓕ He is busy watching a game out the window.
   Ⓖ He is jealous that Kai has a nice gray suit.
   Ⓗ He thinks Kai should have stayed there.
   Ⓘ He knows he will miss Kai very much.

Written Response

9. Explain how you know that Kai is brave. Use information and details from the story to explain your answer.

____

____

____

____

____

TOTAL SCORE: ______ /8 + ______ /2

Name ______________________________

Weekly Lesson Test
Lesson 4

Focus Skill: Compare and Contrast

▶ **Read the passage. Then choose the best answer for each question.**

Cats and Dogs

Vinay's family has two pets—a cat and a dog. Vinay's favorite is Scout, the dog. His sister Sana prefers Princess, the cat. Their parents like both pets equally.

The family pets are similar in some ways. Both of them love to cuddle. They will curl up at Vinay's feet when he sleeps at night, but he has to leave his door open. Also, both Scout and Princess love to play. Vinay can toss a ball and Scout will fetch it. Sana waves a string around and Princess tries to bat it with her paws. But the similarities stop there.

Scout is very loyal. When Vinay gets home from school, the dog is waiting. Vinay thinks cats are too independent, because sometimes Princess hides from Sana. Princess, unlike Scout, doesn't always want to be petted. But Sana likes her cat's independence. It means less work. Cats clean themselves. They do not need to be walked. Dogs, on the other hand, need a lot of attention. They need a walk at least twice a day. Dogs need baths, too, but Vinay doesn't mind. He likes spending time with his dog.

1. Who likes cats better?

   Ⓐ Vinay

   Ⓑ Sana

   Ⓒ their father

   Ⓓ their mother

Name ______________________________

Weekly Lesson Test
Lesson 4

2. What do their pets have in common?
   Ⓕ They love to play.
   Ⓖ They hide a lot.
   Ⓗ They need baths.
   Ⓘ They are independent.

3. How are the pets different?
   Ⓐ The cat plays, but the dog doesn't.
   Ⓑ The dog cleans himself, but the cat needs baths.
   Ⓒ The dog is loyal, but the cat is independent.
   Ⓓ The cat needs walks, but the dog doesn't.

4. Which of the following is true for dogs but not true for cats?
   Ⓕ Dogs clean themselves.
   Ⓖ Dogs often hide.
   Ⓗ Dogs are independent.
   Ⓘ Dogs need a lot of attention.

TOTAL SCORE: ______ /4

Name ______________________________

Robust Vocabulary

Choose the word that best completes each sentence.

1. I _____ my eyes from the bright light to shield them.
   - Ⓐ cringed
   - Ⓑ craned
   - Ⓒ strolled
   - Ⓓ averted

2. Are you _____ me of hiding your book?
   - Ⓕ accusing
   - Ⓖ snickering
   - Ⓗ depriving
   - Ⓘ surrendering

3. The driver was so angry that he could not hide his _____.
   - Ⓐ fluke
   - Ⓑ interrogation
   - Ⓒ queasiness
   - Ⓓ fury

4. Each new president _____ promises to do his duty.
   - Ⓕ particularly
   - Ⓖ solemnly
   - Ⓗ accusingly
   - Ⓘ sternly

5. The police officer had questions to ask, so she put the thief in a room for _____.
   - Ⓐ fury
   - Ⓑ stroll
   - Ⓒ interrogation
   - Ⓓ surrender

Name ______________________________

Weekly Lesson Test
Lesson 4

6. The puppy ______ when the larger dog growled at him.
   Ⓕ muttered
   Ⓖ craned
   Ⓗ foisted
   Ⓘ cringed

7. Tasha was talking during class, and Mr. Young gave her a ______ look.
   Ⓐ stern
   Ⓑ particular
   Ⓒ stunned
   Ⓓ cringed

8. He ______ his neck out the window to see what was happening on the roof.
   Ⓕ cringed
   Ⓖ flinched
   Ⓗ craned
   Ⓘ strolled

TOTAL SCORE: ______ /8

Name ______________________________

Weekly Lesson Test
Lesson 4

Grammar: Complete and Simple Subjects and Predicates

▶ **Choose the best answer for each question.**

1. What is the complete subject in this sentence?

   This morning the sun was shining so brightly.

   Ⓐ This morning
   Ⓑ the sun
   Ⓒ was shining
   Ⓓ so brightly

2. What is the simple predicate in this sentence?

   Before closing the door, her parents waved.

   Ⓕ Before closing
   Ⓖ the door
   Ⓗ her parents
   Ⓘ waved

3. What is the simple subject in this sentence?

   My grandfather's favorite place to fish is Bear Lake.

   Ⓐ Bear Lake
   Ⓑ grandfather's
   Ⓒ place
   Ⓓ to fish

4. What is the complete predicate in this sentence?

   My neighbor does a two-mile run every morning.

   Ⓕ every morning
   Ⓖ during the summer.
   Ⓗ My neighbor
   Ⓘ does a two-mile run

TOTAL SCORE: ______ /4

Name ______________________________

Weekly Lesson Test

Lesson 4

Oral Reading Fluency

At first glance, you may think butterflies and moths may look the same. They both have small bodies, six legs, and four large wings. Their mouths resemble long drinking straws. However, these two kinds of insects are actually quite different from each other.

If you visit a field filled with lush flowers on a sunny day, you have a good chance of seeing butterflies. Butterflies are active during the day, and they receive their nourishment from flowers. They like wide, open spaces with plenty of sunlight.

Butterflies are easy to spot, especially when they have landed on an object and are not moving. Their wings are covered with patterns of vivid colors. When they are resting, they hold their wings straight up or out to the sides.

Unlike butterflies, most moths are active at night. They prefer to be in the forest where it is dark and cool. When they are resting, they fold up their wings, which are usually in a shade of gray or brown.

Moths feed on many different things, including flowers, tree sap, and fruit. Some moths even eat cotton or wool and they may gnaw holes in blankets or clothes that they find in basements, sheds, or closets.

Moths and butterflies can be found in all parts of the world except for places where it is very cold all year round. Next time you are outside, keep your eyes open for one of these interesting insects.

_______ /WCPM

Name ______________________________

Weekly
Lesson Test
Lesson 5

Selection Comprehension

Choose the best answer for each question.

1. What is Pedro's problem in the selection?
   Ⓐ He thinks he must find a special band.
   Ⓑ He wants his grandfather to visit longer.
   Ⓒ He cannot find his grandfather's puppets.
   Ⓓ He doesn't know what to do for his homework.

2. Why is Pedro's mother worried?
   Ⓕ Pedro has a fever.
   Ⓖ Pedro does not eat during dinner.
   Ⓗ Miguel wants to eat Pedro's food.
   Ⓘ Miguel has agreed to help with the play.

3. Why did the author write "Pedro Puts on a Play"?
   Ⓐ to persuade readers to visit Mexico City
   Ⓑ to point out some old Mexican traditions
   Ⓒ to tell how a boy learned about his heritage
   Ⓓ to teach people about their "cultural heritage"

4. Why doesn't Pedro's father like the idea of the mariachi band?
   Ⓕ He has forgotten how to play the music in a band.
   Ⓖ He believes that hiring a band would cost too much.
   Ⓗ He thinks he will have to dress up in a fancy costume.
   Ⓘ He thinks it would be hard to find a band on short notice.

5. What happens RIGHT AFTER Pedro's play?
   Ⓐ The class applauds for Pedro and asks questions.
   Ⓑ Pedro's grandfather explains the Mexican puppets.
   Ⓒ Pedro's father says the puppets are a family treasure.
   Ⓓ Grandfather asks if Pedro's father has forgotten the puppets.

Name ______________________________

Weekly Lesson Test
Lesson 5

6. With which sentence would Pedro's grandfather be MOST LIKELY to agree?
   Ⓕ Children should know about family traditions.
   Ⓖ Students should do their homework on the weekends.
   Ⓗ People should be careful where they put family treasures.
   Ⓘ Parents should often put on puppet shows with their children.

7. Which action BEST shows that Pedro feels proud of his heritage?
   Ⓐ Pedro finds his father's toy puppets.
   Ⓑ Pedro tells Mrs. Lloyd that his skills run in the family.
   Ⓒ Pedro asks Miguel to help him put on a play.
   Ⓓ Pedro will not eat dinner.

8. Which is an example of "cultural heritage"?
   Ⓕ a basketball game
   Ⓖ a cake from a bakery
   Ⓗ a quilt made by an aunt
   Ⓘ a recipe from a cookbook

Written Response

9. How do Pedro's feelings change in the selection? Explain how his feelings change and why.

____

____

____

____

TOTAL SCORE: ______ /8 + ______ /2

Name ______________________________

Weekly Lesson Test
Lesson 5

Robust Vocabulary

Choose the word that best completes each sentence.

1. My uncle cooks, and this is his favorite ______ supply store.
   Ⓐ culinary
   Ⓑ vivid
   Ⓒ reminiscent
   Ⓓ downcast

2. After seeing such a sad movie, Keisha felt ______.
   Ⓕ extensive
   Ⓖ vivid
   Ⓗ reminiscent
   Ⓘ downcast

3. The difficult math problem was a source of great ______.
   Ⓐ fury
   Ⓑ cringing
   Ⓒ consternation
   Ⓓ interrogation

4. The roses in the painting are so ______ that I can almost smell them.
   Ⓕ stern
   Ⓖ vivid
   Ⓗ pensive
   Ⓘ downcast

5. Mr. Ramos has been a carpenter for years, so he has ______ experience in building houses.
   Ⓐ vivid
   Ⓑ pensive
   Ⓒ downcast
   Ⓓ extensive

Name ___

6. Rhonda seemed very calm as she sat _____ on the park bench.
   (F) serenely
   (G) furiously
   (H) accusingly
   (I) extensively

7. The unforgettable smell of fresh bread is _____ of my father's bakery.
   (A) pensive
   (B) downcast
   (C) reminiscent
   (D) extensive

8. Jack looked _____ as he tried to make a decision.
   (F) pensive
   (G) reminiscent
   (H) extensive
   (I) vivid

9. Our club will try to _____ new members next year.
   (A) interrogate
   (B) recruit
   (C) cringe
   (D) accuse

10. The ball game _____ with the national anthem.
   (F) averted
   (G) cringed
   (H) commenced
   (I) accused

TOTAL SCORE: _____ /10

Name ______________________________

Weekly Lesson Test
Lesson 6

Selection Comprehension

Directions: Chose the best answer for each question.

1. Which idea BEST shows that going to town is important?
   Ⓐ Pa walks beside the oxen.
   Ⓑ Ma packs a lunch for the trip.
   Ⓒ Ma makes new clothes for Carrie.
   Ⓓ Pa says they will return before sundown.

2. What is the girl's BIGGEST problem in the story?
   Ⓕ The cattle get into the hay-stacks.
   Ⓖ The girls have to wash their dishes.
   Ⓗ Mary will not let Laura play outside.
   Ⓘ The girls cannot go to the swimming hole.

3. Laura MOST LIKELY says she likes wolves more than cattle because wolves
   Ⓐ are smaller than cows.
   Ⓑ hunt their own food.
   Ⓒ are smarter than cows.
   Ⓓ have interesting howls.

4. Why does Laura shout at Johnny Johnson?
   Ⓕ to remind him to put the cattle in the barn
   Ⓖ to warn him to pay attention to the cattle
   Ⓗ to tell him Pa and Ma will be home soon
   Ⓘ to explain what happened by the hay-stacks

5. Why do Laura and Mary argue?
   Ⓐ Laura wants Mary to milk Spot.
   Ⓑ Laura wants to help Ma make supper.
   Ⓒ Mary wants Laura to stay away from the cattle.
   Ⓓ Mary wants Laura to obey her because she's older.

Name ______________________________

Weekly Lesson Test
Lesson 6

6. Compared with Mary, Laura is
   Ⓕ bolder.
   Ⓖ smarter.
   Ⓗ more honest.
   Ⓘ more honest.

7. After Pa saves Ma and Carrie, why do the girls hug Ma tightly?
   Ⓐ They feel grateful that Ma is safe.
   Ⓑ They are angry that Ma frightened them.
   Ⓒ They want to keep Ma from leaving again.
   Ⓓ They want Ma to protect them from the oxen.

8. How do you know that this story is historical fiction?
   Ⓕ It teaches a lesson or moral about life.
   Ⓖ The characters are not like real people.
   Ⓗ The story events could not happen in real life.
   Ⓘ It takes place at a real time and place in the past.

Written Response

9. **COMPARING TEXTS** What problems did the pioneers face on the Great Plains? Use details from BOTH "Surviving on the Prairie" and "On the Banks of Plum Creek" to support your answer.

____

____

____

____

____

TOTAL SCORE: ______ /8 + ______ /2

Name ______________________________

Weekly Lesson Test
Lesson 6

Focus Skill: Plot: Conflict and Resolution

Read the passage. Then choose the best answer for each question.

The Promise

Last week, Li Mei had promised Mrs. Landon that she would babysit on Saturday. As luck would have it, on Saturday morning Jodie, Li Mei's friend, called and invited Li Mei to go to the fair. It was the last day of the fair, and Li Mei really wanted to go.

She thought about her promise to Mrs. Landon. Maybe she could offer to take the twins to the fair. Li Mei worked out the details of her plan. Then she called Mrs. Landon, but Li Mei did not get a chance to talk.

"The twins are sick," said Mrs. Landon. "I'm sorry to change plans, but I will not need a babysitter today after all."

1. What does Li Mei promise?
   - Ⓐ She promises to babysit Mrs. Landon's twins.
   - Ⓑ She promises to go to the fair with Jodie.
   - Ⓒ She promises to take the twins to the fair.
   - Ⓓ She promises to call Mrs. Landon with a plan.

2. What problem does Li Mei have?
   - Ⓕ Li Mei has promised to babysit, but the twins are sick.
   - Ⓖ Mrs. Landon will not allow the twins to go to the fair.
   - Ⓗ Li Mei wants to go to the fair, but she has promised to babysit.
   - Ⓘ Mrs. Landon does not allow Li Mei to talk on the phone.

Name ______________________________

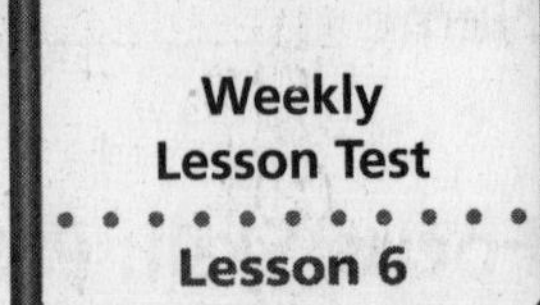

3. How does Li Mei plan to deal with the conflict?

Ⓐ She will offer to babysit the twins another day.

Ⓑ She will offer to take the twins to the fair.

Ⓒ She will ask Jodie to help her babysit the twins.

Ⓓ She will tell Jodie she cannot go to the fair.

4. How is the conflict resolved?

Ⓕ Mrs. Landon does not need a babysitter after all.

Ⓖ Jodie offers to babysit so Li Mei can go to the fair.

Ⓗ Jodie cannot go to the fair after all.

Ⓘ Mrs. Landon accepts Li Mei's plan.

TOTAL SCORE: ______ /4

Name ______________________________

Prefixes, Suffixes, and Roots

Choose the best answer for each question.

1. Read this sentence.

    Maria likes different colors now, so she wants to redecorate her room.

    What is the meaning of the word *redecorate*?

    Ⓐ decorate again
    Ⓑ not decorate
    Ⓒ able to be decorated
    Ⓓ decorate before

2. Read this sentence.

    As motionless as a statue, the turtle sat on the log.

    What is the meaning of the word *motionless*?

    Ⓕ full of motion
    Ⓖ able to be in motion
    Ⓗ without motion
    Ⓘ in motion again

3. Read this sentence.

    Those ripe strawberries I ate were juicy and flavorful.

    What is the meaning of the word *flavorful*?

    Ⓐ having flavor again
    Ⓑ having flavor before
    Ⓒ without flavor
    Ⓓ full of flavor

Name ____________________

Weekly Lesson Test
Lesson 6

4. Read this sentence.

All of the inexpensive games are stacked on the sale table.

What is the meaning of the word *inexpensive*?

Ⓕ not expensive
Ⓖ expensive again
Ⓗ expensive before
Ⓘ able to be expensive

TOTAL SCORE: ______ /4

Name ______________________________

Weekly Lesson Test
Lesson 6

Robust Vocabulary

Choose the word that best completes each sentence.

1. When the mouse ran across the kitchen floor, my cat Fluffy _____ on it.
   - Ⓐ pounced
   - Ⓑ darted
   - Ⓒ swerved
   - Ⓓ commenced

2. My mother said I was _____ for making my lunch.
   - Ⓕ pensive
   - Ⓖ downcast
   - Ⓗ responsible
   - Ⓘ attentive

3. The zoo was so crowded that visitors were _____ each other to see the rare animals.
   - Ⓐ contradicting
   - Ⓑ jostling
   - Ⓒ reminiscent
   - Ⓓ pensive

4. My little brother is always _____ me when I give my opinions about baseball teams.
   - Ⓕ contradicting
   - Ⓖ recruiting
   - Ⓗ jostling
   - Ⓘ sparkling

Name ______________________________

Weekly Lesson Test
Lesson 6

5. The car _____ to avoid the falling rocks.

Ⓐ swerved
Ⓑ recruited
Ⓒ pounced
Ⓓ commenced

6. The lizard _____ across the busy road.

Ⓕ commenced
Ⓖ pounced
Ⓗ recruited
Ⓘ darted

7. To get good grades, one should be _____ in class.

Ⓐ downcast
Ⓑ vivid
Ⓒ attentive
Ⓓ extensive

TOTAL SCORE: _____ /7

Name ______________________________

Weekly Lesson Test
Lesson 6

Grammar: Compound Subjects and Predicates

▶ **Choose the best answer for each question.**

1. Read the sentences.

   Mia loves to sing. Mia loves to dance. Mia loves to swim.

   Which is the best compound predicate for combining the three sentences?

   Ⓕ sings, dances, and swims
   Ⓖ loves to sing, dance, and swim
   Ⓗ loves to sing, dance, or swim
   Ⓘ sing and dance

2. Read the sentences.

   Bats are able to fly. Birds are able to fly. Bees are able to fly.

   Which is the best compound subject for combining the three sentences?

   Ⓐ Bats, birds, and bees
   Ⓑ Bats and birds
   Ⓒ Bats or birds and bees
   Ⓓ Bats, birds, or bees

3. Read the sentences.

   Diego is tall. Mac is tall. Jon is also tall.

   Which is the best way to combine the sentences into one sentence?

   Ⓕ Diego, Mac, or Jon is tall.
   Ⓖ Diego and Mac and Jon are tall.
   Ⓗ Diego, Mac, and Jon are tall.
   Ⓘ Diego, Mac, and Jon is tall.

TOTAL SCORE: _____ /3

Name ______________________________

Weekly
Lesson Test
Lesson 6

Oral Reading Fluency

Bradley couldn't believe that his best friend was moving, and that his friend wasn't just moving to another school across town or to another city. He wasn't even moving to another state. His best friend was moving to another country.

Bradley and Mehul had been best friends since they met on the first day of first grade. That was the year that Mehul's family had arrived from India. And now three years later, they were moving back there. Mehul's grandparents still lived in India, and they were getting older and needed someone to help them with their health care. Because of this, Mehul's parents wanted to live closer to them. It would also be an opportunity for Mehul and his sister Falguni to learn more about India and their ethnic heritage. The family would stay in India for only a year or two, as long as it took to prepare Mehul's grandparents for their move to the United States, but when you're ten years old, that is an especially long time. In two years, Bradley would be in middle school. Bradley could not imagine what life without Mehul would be like.

Bradley and his mother went to Mehul's house to tell the family good-bye. Bradley presented Mehul with a baseball autographed by their favorite player. Mehul gave Bradley his trampoline for safekeeping. It was much too large for them to take halfway around the globe. Bradley agreed to take care of it while Mehul was in India. Upon Mehul's return, Bradley promised to return the trampoline to him. But Bradley told Mehul the baseball was his to keep.

_______ /WCPM

Name ______________________________________

Weekly Lesson Test
Lesson 7

Selection Comprehension

Chose the best answer for each question.

1. What is Justin's MAIN conflict with himself?
   Ⓐ He is ashamed because he cannot do chores perfectly.
   Ⓑ He wishes he could cook like Grandpa.
   Ⓒ He worries about his clothes for the festival.
   Ⓓ He thinks nobody should ever do housework.

2. Which fact BEST shows that Justin may have been to the ranch before?
   Ⓕ He agrees to ride fence with Grandpa.
   Ⓖ He knows how to saddle and ride Black.
   Ⓗ He is excited about going to the festival.
   Ⓘ He is surprised when Grandpa puts flour in a pan.

3. What happens RIGHT AFTER Pal starts drinking at the stream?
   Ⓐ Justin hears a noise in the grass.
   Ⓑ Justin sees a fawn stuck in the fence.
   Ⓒ Justin watches Grandpa make biscuits.
   Ⓓ Justin asks Grandpa about Black cowboys.

4. With which sentence would Grandpa MOST LIKELY agree?
   Ⓕ Cooking and cleaning are women's work.
   Ⓖ Boys should learn how to rope and ride bulls.
   Ⓗ Doing the dishes is a lot of fun.
   Ⓘ It is important to learn to do chores the best we can.

5. Why does Grandpa say, "Tears bathe the soul"?
   Ⓐ He thinks Justin saw him crying.
   Ⓑ He wants Justin to tell him about someone who cried.
   Ⓒ He wants Justin to take a bath.
   Ⓓ He wants Justin to realize that crying is all right.

Name ___________________________

Weekly Lesson Test
Lesson 7

6. Why did the author write the story "Justin and the Best Biscuits in the World"?
   Ⓕ to tell readers about life on a ranch
   Ⓖ to teach readers how to make good biscuits
   Ⓗ to teach readers about work and self-confidence
   Ⓘ to explain to readers about cowboys in the Old West

7. Which sentence BEST states a main theme of the story?
   Ⓐ The life of a cowboy is often lonely.
   Ⓑ Staying busy keeps people from feeling worried.
   Ⓒ People can do any job if they put their mind to it.
   Ⓓ It is usually best to keep your feelings to yourself.

8. How do you know that this story is realistic fiction?
   Ⓕ The characters act like real people.
   Ⓖ The events do not seem real.
   Ⓗ It gives facts and information about a subject.
   Ⓘ It has characters who must solve a mystery.

Written Response

9. What did Grandpa do to help Justin feel better about himself? Use details and information from "Justin and the Best Biscuits in the World" to support your answer.

____

____

____

____

TOTAL SCORE: _______ /8 + _______ /2

Name ______________________________

Weekly Lesson Test
Lesson 7

Focus Skill: Plot: Conflict and Resolution

Read the passage. Then choose the best answer for each question.

The Missing Dog

Ever since he was eight years old, Mark had operated his own pet care business. His neighbors' pets all loved him. Mark loved taking care of them, too, until the day that he arrived at Ms. Khan's house to find the gate open and Ms. Khan's little dog, Mopsy, gone.

With Ms. Khan away on business that day, Mopsy was Mark's responsibility. Mark walked though the neighborhood calling Mopsy's name and asking neighbors whether they had seen Mopsy, but no one had. For a long time, Mark sat at the open gate waiting for Mopsy with fresh food, but she did not return. It was starting to get late, and Mark needed to go home. With shoulders hunched and head down, Mark started toward home. As he approached his house, he heard a familiar bark. Mopsy was waiting at Mark's front door!

1. Which is the first sign that Mark is going to have a problem?
   - Ⓐ Ms. Khan is away on business.
   - Ⓑ Neighborhood pets love Mark.
   - Ⓒ Ms. Khan's gate is open.
   - Ⓓ Mark hears Mopsy's bark.

2. What problem does Mark have to solve?
   - Ⓕ He cannot find enough customers for his business.
   - Ⓖ He has too many dogs to feed.
   - Ⓗ He cannot find one of the dogs he is taking care of.
   - Ⓘ He has too little time to take care of Mopsy.

Name ___________________________________

Weekly Lesson Test

Lesson 7

3. How does Mark try to solve his problem?

Ⓐ He calls Ms. Khan.

Ⓑ He looks for Mopsy.

Ⓒ He goes straight home.

Ⓓ He repairs the gate.

4. How is the conflict resolved?

Ⓕ Mopsy is waiting for Mark at Mark's house.

Ⓖ Mark finds Mopsy at a neighbor's house.

Ⓗ Mopsy comes home when she smells fresh food.

Ⓘ Mark waits until Mopsy comes back to the open gate.

TOTAL SCORE: ______ /4

Name ______________________________

Weekly Lesson Test
Lesson 7

Prefixes, Suffixes, and Roots

Choose the best answer for each question.

1. What is the root word of *actually*?

Ⓐ act
Ⓑ actual
Ⓒ ally
Ⓓ ly

2. Which of the following is the suffix in the word *objection*?

Ⓕ ob-
Ⓖ -ject
Ⓗ object
Ⓘ -ion

3. Read this sentence.

Our volleyball team did so well this season that they were unequaled.

What is the meaning of the word *unequaled*?

Ⓐ with many equals
Ⓑ with no equals
Ⓒ equaled before
Ⓓ equaled again

Name ______________________________

Weekly Lesson Test
Lesson 7

4. Read this sentence.

   In science class, the students were studying poisonous snakes.

   What is the meaning of the word *poisonous*?

   Ⓕ with no poison
   Ⓖ having poison
   Ⓗ having little poison
   Ⓘ turning into poison

5. Read this sentence.

   As Dr. Patel poked on Jason's injured knee, the knee's soreness increased.

   What is the meaning of the word *soreness*?

   Ⓐ state of feeling too much pain
   Ⓑ state of feeling no pain
   Ⓒ state of feeling pain
   Ⓓ state of accepting pain

TOTAL SCORE: ______ /5

Name ______________________________

Robust Vocabulary

Choose the word that best completes each sentence.

1. My sister sleeps in her clothes, so they always look _____.
   (A) rumpled
   (B) resounded
   (C) untangled
   (D) reluctant

2. Even at the back of the schoolyard the tardy bell _____ loudly.
   (F) darted
   (G) lurked
   (H) resounded
   (I) pounced

3. The tightrope walker makes sure that the rope is _____ before each performance.
   (A) rumpled
   (B) attentive
   (C) reluctant
   (D) taut

4. A raccoon _____ in the alley, looking for open garbage cans.
   (F) untangled
   (G) lurked
   (H) rumpled
   (I) surged

Name ______________________________

Weekly Lesson Test
Lesson 7

5. It took me an hour to get all the strings _____ from the huge knot.
Ⓐ untangled
Ⓑ surged
Ⓒ rumpled
Ⓓ resounded

6. As soon as I put my hand in the icy water, a _____ of tingling pain went through my arm.
Ⓕ recruit
Ⓖ surge
Ⓗ lurk
Ⓘ swerve

7. My older brother used to be _____ to do his chores.
Ⓐ taut
Ⓑ rumpled
Ⓒ resounded
Ⓓ reluctant

8. As soon as the detectives arrived, they began _____ the crime scene.
Ⓕ contradicting
Ⓖ jostling
Ⓗ inspecting
Ⓘ surging

TOTAL SCORE: _____ /8

Name ______________________________

Weekly Lesson Test
Lesson 7

Grammar: Simple and Compound Sentences

Choose the best answer for each question.

1. Which is a simple sentence?

   Ⓐ Mr. Parker is in school, but his class is on a field trip.
   Ⓑ Mr. Parker's class is on a field trip to the science museum.
   Ⓒ Mr. Parker's class is on a field trip, but they will be back soon.
   Ⓓ Is Mr. Parker in school, or is he on the field trip to the museum?

2. Which is a compound sentence?

   Ⓕ Katia and Emilia went to the circus.
   Ⓖ Katia and Emilia went to the circus and ate dinner out.
   Ⓗ Katia went to the circus, but Emilia ate dinner out.
   Ⓘ Katia went to the circus and ate dinner out with Emilia.

3. Read the sentences.

   Thomas Edison was an inventor. Alexander Calder was an artist.

   Which is the best way to combine these sentences?

   Ⓐ Thomas Edison was an inventor, but Alexander Calder was an artist.
   Ⓑ Thomas Edison and Alexander Calder were inventors and artists.
   Ⓒ Thomas Edison was an inventor, for Alexander Calder was an artist.
   Ⓓ Thomas Edison and Alexander Calder was an inventor and an artist.

TOTAL SCORE: ______ /3

Name ____________________

Weekly Lesson Test

Lesson 7

Oral Reading Fluency

You have probably heard about scientific studies indicating that breakfast is the most important meal of the day. Unfortunately, breakfast is also a meal that many people tend to skip, and skipping breakfast affects the body. It can even affect how people learn.

For more than 50 years, scientists have been studying the effects of breakfast on the brain. What have they found? Children who do not eat breakfast cannot remember things as well as children who do eat breakfast. The breakfast skippers also make more mistakes than the breakfast eaters.

What did you eat for breakfast today? It really matters. You probably already know that sugary cereals are not the best choice. However, scientists wanted to make sure. They compared students who ate a sugary cereal for breakfast with students who ate oatmeal with sugar. The same amount of sugar was contained in both breakfasts. Can you guess which group did better? The oatmeal eaters did. In fact, they did a great deal better.

Sugary cereals give the body quick energy. Oatmeal gives the body energy more slowly. When the body has energy throughout the morning, it can work better until lunchtime. So the best breakfast foods are those that supply energy slowly all morning. A whole-grain cereal with milk is a good choice.

_______ /WCPM

Name ____________________

Weekly Lesson Test
Lesson 8

Selection Comprehension

▶ **Choose the best answer for each question.**

1. How can you tell that "The Three Little Cyberpigs" is a play?
   (A) It has characters and action.
   (B) It has a problem to be solved.
   (C) It has dialogue and stage directions.
   (D) It has a beginning, a middle, and an end.

2. Where does most of the play take place?
   (F) at a grocery store
   (G) in a computer shop
   (H) at the three pigs' house
   (I) in a children's bookstore

3. This play is MAINLY about three pigs who
   (A) learn about what computers can do.
   (B) cannot start their computer programs.
   (C) help others solve computer problems.
   (D) try to send an email message on a computer.

4. How does Ann help the pigs?
   (F) She guides them through the cybershop.
   (G) She shows them how to write nursery rhymes.
   (H) She teaches them to make sound effects.
   (I) She warns them that the wolf is nearby.

5. Why does P.J. say they should leave the store?
   (A) He wants to help Little Bo Peep find her sheep.
   (B) He has found his disk.
   (C) He has learned all about computers.
   (D) He does not want the wolf to destroy the store.

Name ______________________________

6. How is the main conflict in the play finally resolved?
   Ⓕ The pigs frighten the wolf away.
   Ⓖ Ann tames the wolf.
   Ⓗ The wolf gets erased by the characters.
   Ⓘ The wolf is put in a file by Miss Muffet.

7. How can Ann BEST be described?
   Ⓐ threatening
   Ⓑ worried
   Ⓒ polite
   Ⓓ helpful

8. How do you know that the author of this play likes computers?
   Ⓕ All the characters talk in rhymes.
   Ⓖ All the characters say good things about computers.
   Ⓗ The play is set in a computer store.
   Ⓘ The virus is destroyed in the end.

Written Response

9. In what ways are the pigs and the other characters in the play ALIKE? How are they different? Use details and information from "The Three Little Cyberpigs" to support your answer.

____

____

____

____

____

TOTAL SCORE: ______ /8 + ______ /2

Name ______________________________

Focus Skill: Author's Purpose and Perspective

Read the passage. Then choose the best answer for each question.

Recycling

Recycling is the process of using materials again. The process begins with the collection of materials that can be recycled, like plastic, paper, or glass, from residences and businesses. The materials are then used to make new products. The new products make their way to store shelves, where we buy them, use them, and hopefully recycle them again.

The main reason to recycle is to take care of the environment. Wasting materials that could be reused can leave permanent damage to our planet. Cutting down trees, for example, to make new paper while used paper is going into landfills is a bad idea. If it continues, we may lose some of our forests, and our land will be filled with waste paper.

People can and should do their share. Although more people than ever before are recycling, much more remains to be done. Less than thirty percent of the garbage in the United States is recycled, yet officials present this figure as a great accomplishment. Would you be happy with a thirty on your report card?

1. What is the author's main purpose?
   - Ⓐ to entertain people who recycle
   - Ⓑ to inform companies about recycling programs
   - Ⓒ to persuade people to recycle
   - Ⓓ to teach companies a lesson on recycling

2. What is the author's main purpose in the first paragraph?
   Ⓕ to entertain the audience with jokes
   Ⓖ to inform the audience of basic facts
   Ⓗ to persuade the audience to recycle
   Ⓘ to teach the audience a moral lesson

3. How does the author feel about recycling?
   Ⓐ She thinks recycling is a waste of time.
   Ⓑ She thinks more recycling should be done.
   Ⓒ She thinks recycling is destroying forests.
   Ⓓ She thinks less recycling will occur in the future.

4. Why do you think the author included the last line?
   Ⓕ to encourage readers to set higher goals for recycling rates
   Ⓖ to discourage readers from recycling
   Ⓗ to encourage readers to get bad grades
   Ⓘ to discourage readers from trusting official figures about recycling

TOTAL SCORE: ______ /4

Name ______________________________

Weekly Lesson Test
Lesson 8

Locate Information

Choose the best answer for each question.

1. Which is the best way to search a library database for books by Beverly Cleary?
   Ⓐ by book title
   Ⓑ by author's name
   Ⓒ by keyword
   Ⓓ by call number

2. Where would you search to find recent information about new models of bicycles?
   Ⓕ a CD-ROM encyclopedia
   Ⓖ the Internet
   Ⓗ a CD-ROM dictionary
   Ⓘ a library database

3. Which of the following could you most easily research by using a CD-ROM encyclopedia?
   Ⓐ today's weather
   Ⓑ current sports scores
   Ⓒ photographs of your town's courthouse
   Ⓓ life history of a former U.S. president

4. What information would you most easily find on a local newspaper's website?
   Ⓕ information about the latest game in the World Series
   Ⓖ information about different breeds of dogs
   Ⓗ the population of Tampa, Florida
   Ⓘ the length of the Mississippi River

TOTAL SCORE: ______ /4

Name ____________________________________

Weekly Lesson Test
Lesson 8

Robust Vocabulary

▶ **Choose the word that best completes each sentence.**

1. Cecilia's new silver and blue bicycle is fast and ______.

Ⓐ reluctant
Ⓑ impressed
Ⓒ slick
Ⓓ taut

2. My dad does stretching exercises daily, so he was ______ enough to avoid the falling paint can.

Ⓕ fierce
Ⓖ nimble
Ⓗ taut
Ⓘ impressed

3. Although our dog sounds ______ when he growls, he is actually very gentle.

Ⓐ nimble
Ⓑ slick
Ⓒ taut
Ⓓ fierce

4. Saber-toothed tigers no longer ______ on Earth; they are extinct.

Ⓕ exist
Ⓖ cease
Ⓗ resound
Ⓘ surge

Name ____

Weekly Lesson Test
Lesson 8

5. Some people are so _____ with new technology that they rush to purchase it.

   Ⓐ impressed
   Ⓑ ceased
   Ⓒ lurked
   Ⓓ resounded

6. The people at the loud party were asked to _____ making noise that disturbed the neighbors.

   Ⓕ surge
   Ⓖ cease
   Ⓗ exist
   Ⓘ lurk

TOTAL SCORE: _______ /6

Name ______________________________

Weekly Lesson Test
Lesson 8

Grammar: Prepositional Phrases

▶ **Choose the best answer for each question.**

1. Read this sentence.

   Ben and his friends like sleeping late in the morning.

   Which is the preposition in the sentence?

   Ⓐ and
   Ⓑ his
   Ⓒ in
   Ⓓ the

2. Read this sentence.

   The crowd cheered as Shakila kicked the soccer ball into the goal.

   Which is the prepositional phrase in the sentence?

   Ⓕ The crowd cheered
   Ⓖ as Shakila kicked
   Ⓗ the soccer ball
   Ⓘ into the goal

3. Read this sentence.

   Mr. Campo served the soup _____ a large ladle.

   Which preposition best completes the sentence?

   Ⓐ near
   Ⓑ with
   Ⓒ around
   Ⓓ under

Name ____________________

4. Read this sentence.

The dog ran in circles _____ the tree.

Which preposition best completes the sentence?

Ⓕ off

Ⓖ above

Ⓗ around

Ⓘ with

TOTAL SCORE: _____ /4

Name ______________________________

Weekly Lesson Test
Lesson 8

Oral Reading Fluency

Vera quietly read the newspaper article that her father had clipped and left for her to read at breakfast. As she read, she felt a lump form in her throat. How could the city plan to construct a busy street through their neighborhood park?

She and her friends loved the park's beautiful, tall trees. They explored there often, following trails through the trees. Sometimes they found animal tracks, which they thought belonged to deer. Most of all, they simply relaxed there, and enjoyed having nature around them. The park was an ideal place to hang out after school.

Now the city was going to build a major street that would divide the park in half. Trees would be cut down, pavement would replace the grass, and fast cars would zip through the park.

Vera wanted to do something to change the city's mind. She talked to her friends about the road construction plans. Together, they started writing letters to the city, explaining why the park was important to them, to the animals, and to the city.

When the letters didn't work, Vera started a petition. She sent it to schools all over her city and collected more than 20,000 signatures. She and other children took the petition to City Hall. The City Council was very impressed with the children's work, and the city decided to build the new street around the park instead of through it.

_______ /WCPM

Name ____

Weekly
Lesson Test
Lesson 9

Selection Comprehension

▶ Choose the best answer for each question.

1. What is the MAIN reason the author wrote this selection?
   Ⓐ to persuade readers to make baskets
   Ⓑ to show why baskets are hard to make
   Ⓒ to explain an ancient art form
   Ⓓ to tell about a basket-weaving event

2. How do you know that this selection is expository nonfiction?
   Ⓕ It tells about the author's thoughts.
   Ⓖ It gives information about a topic.
   Ⓗ It presents a solution to a problem.
   Ⓘ It has some made-up events and people.

3. According to the selection, what is the FIRST step in making a basket?
   Ⓐ peeling the roots
   Ⓑ scraping the bark
   Ⓒ twisting the string
   Ⓓ gathering the plants

4. Which sentence is an OPINION from the selection?
   Ⓕ They are *really* sour—worse than a dill pickle!
   Ⓖ There are two ways of making baskets: coiling and twining.
   Ⓗ Geography and climate determine an area's plant life.
   Ⓘ Beginners, young or old, learn from more experienced weavers.

5. How does the author feel about California Indian weaving?
   Ⓐ Weaving a design is a simple task.
   Ⓑ Young weavers should carry on the tradition.
   Ⓒ Weaving is the most difficult skill to learn.
   Ⓓ The prettiest baskets are made by adult weavers.

Name ____

Weekly
Lesson Test
Lesson 9

6. According to the selection, why do California weavers have trouble getting good basket materials?
   Ⓕ People have stopped planting bunchgrass.
   Ⓖ Insects have been destroying the deergrass.
   Ⓗ Harsh winter frosts have damaged the plants.
   Ⓘ People are not allowed to burn fields yearly to help plants.

7. Why do most weavers make only a few baskets each year?
   Ⓐ There are very few Indian tribes in California.
   Ⓑ Indian basket-makers have kept their skill secret.
   Ⓒ Gathering and weaving materials takes a long time.
   Ⓓ The basket-makers' gathering is no longer in California.

8. Why is Carly's Mom working with the Forest Service?
   Ⓕ She needs their help to keep plants healthy.
   Ⓖ She wants to teach them about different plants.
   Ⓗ She worries fires will wipe out native grasses.
   Ⓘ She needs their help gathering supplies on private lands.

Written Response

9. Describe what Carly does at the California Indian Basketweavers Gathering. Explain how these activities help carry on the tribes' traditions. Use information and details from "Weaving a California Tradition" to support your answer.

____

____

____

____

TOTAL SCORE: ______ /8 + ______ /2

Name ____

Weekly
Lesson Test
Lesson 9

Focus Skill: Author's Purpose and Perspective

Read the passage. Then choose the best answer for each question.

Sharifa's Hero

"Write an essay about someone who is a hero in your life," Ms. Bills had said to the class. For the subject of her essay, Sharifa chose her father, because he had taught her many important lessons. One lesson was about hard work, for her father had worked long evenings and most weekends to be able to open his own restaurant. That restaurant now attracted customers from many parts of the city who came to eat her father's unique cooking. He had also taught her not to fear taking risks. When her father decided to leave his home country to come to the United States, his friends at home thought he was foolish. But he proved them wrong. Sharifa thought her father was one of the bravest people in the world.

After Sharifa turned in her essay, Ms. Bills said that she could tell how much Sharifa admired her father. But when Sharifa told her father about what she had written, he could not understand why she would call him a hero. In fact, he was embarrassed. "I am not a hero; I am only an ordinary man," he declared. "I have never saved anyone's life!"

Confused by her father's reaction, Sharifa told her father how glad she was that he had taken risks and worked hard to give her a good life. She wanted him to know that these actions were heroic to her.

Later that night, her father came into her room to say good night. "You really are a hero, Dad," Sharifa said.

"I guess ordinary people can be heroes, too," her father smiled.

Name ______________________________

Weekly
Lesson Test
Lesson 9

1. What is the author's main purpose?
   Ⓐ to teach readers a lesson about what being a hero means
   Ⓑ to inform readers about writing an essay about heroes
   Ⓒ to persuade readers to honor their parents
   Ⓓ to entertain readers with a funny story

2. What is the author's purpose in the first paragraph?
   Ⓕ to explain why Sharifa's father was embarrassed
   Ⓖ to explain why Sharifa chose her father as her hero
   Ⓗ to explain why Sharifa's teacher liked the essay
   Ⓘ to explain how to choose a good topic for a essay

3. Which words from the passage show that the author admires Sharifa's father?
   Ⓐ his friends back home thought he was foolish
   Ⓑ he proved them wrong
   Ⓒ she could tell how much Sharifa admired her father
   Ⓓ he was embarrassed

4. Why do you think the author included the last line?
   Ⓕ to show that Sharifa's father understood why she called him a hero
   Ⓖ to explain why Sharifa's father was puzzled about being called a hero
   Ⓗ to summarize the reasons why Sharifa wrote about her father
   Ⓘ to describe Sharifa's feelings about her father's hard work

TOTAL SCORE: ______ /4

Name ________________________________

Weekly Lesson Test
Lesson 9

Locate Information

Choose the best answer for each question.

1. Which is the best way to find a book titled *Spot a Cat* in a library database?
   Ⓐ by book title
   Ⓑ by author name
   Ⓒ by the keyword *cat*
   Ⓓ by call number

2. Where would you search to find the location of Happy, Texas?
   Ⓕ a CD-ROM encyclopedia
   Ⓖ an online newspaper database
   Ⓗ a CD-ROM atlas
   Ⓘ Internet links on the library web site

3. Which would be the best way to search in a CD-ROM encyclopedia for information about Finland?
   Ⓐ by the letter F
   Ⓑ by author name
   Ⓒ by book title
   Ⓓ by Internet link

4. Which of the following could you most easily research by using a CD-ROM encyclopedia?
   Ⓕ a bus schedule
   Ⓖ this year's top movies
   Ⓗ the giant octopus
   Ⓘ current candidates for an election

Name ______________________________

Weekly Lesson Test
Lesson 9

5. If you wanted to find books about the history of baseball in a library database, which of the following should you do?
   Ⓐ look through the call numbers of books about sports
   Ⓑ type in the keywords "baseball" and "history"
   Ⓒ search for the author name "Baseball Historian"
   Ⓓ look for books with the word "history" in their name

TOTAL SCORE: ______ /5

Name ___________________________

Weekly Lesson Test
Lesson 9

Robust Vocabulary

▶ **Choose the word that best completes each sentence.**

1. After going through difficult times together, Olivia and her mother developed a close _____.
   Ⓐ preserve
   Ⓑ surge
   Ⓒ bond
   Ⓓ interval

2. To protect the _____ glass, Ramon wrapped it carefully in tissue paper.
   Ⓕ nimble
   Ⓖ fierce
   Ⓗ flexible
   Ⓘ delicate

3. Termites are known to _____ rotting trees in the forest.
   Ⓐ cease
   Ⓑ infest
   Ⓒ exist
   Ⓓ inspire

4. Many families use photographs to _____ memories of their favorite events.
   Ⓕ infest
   Ⓖ preserve
   Ⓗ cease
   Ⓘ exist

Name ______________________________

Weekly Lesson Test
Lesson 9

5. Readers usually want to know what _____ authors to write books.
   - Ⓐ inspires
   - Ⓑ ceases
   - Ⓒ infests
   - Ⓓ preserves

6. Jaime's family has a _____ recipe for salsa that they keep secret.
   - Ⓕ flexible
   - Ⓖ reluctant
   - Ⓗ unique
   - Ⓘ nimble

7. The class bell rings at regular _____.
   - Ⓐ preserves
   - Ⓑ slicks
   - Ⓒ bonds
   - Ⓓ intervals

8. A _____ substance such as rubber can be easily bent.
   - Ⓕ flexible
   - Ⓖ delicate
   - Ⓗ fierce
   - Ⓘ unique

TOTAL SCORE: _____ /8

Name ______________________________

Weekly Lesson Test
Lesson 9

Grammar: Clauses and Phrases: Complex Sentences

Choose the best answer for each question.

1. Which of the following is a complex sentence?

   Ⓐ The leaves on the old maple tree turned bright yellow last fall.

   Ⓑ When the weather became cool, the maple leaves turned yellow.

   Ⓒ Last Fall at the park, we saw many brightly colored trees.

   Ⓓ The weather became cold, and the maple leaves turned yellow.

2. Read the sentence.

   After it ate for many days, the caterpillar formed a cocoon and changed into a monarch butterfly.

   Which is the dependent clause in the sentence?

   Ⓕ After it ate for many days

   Ⓖ the caterpillar formed a cocoon

   Ⓗ changed into a monarch butterfly

   Ⓘ the caterpillar formed a cocoon and changed into a monarch butterfly

3. Read the sentences.

   I am hungry again.
   I just finished lunch.

   Which is the best way to combine the sentences into one complex sentence?

   Ⓐ I am hungry again because I just finished lunch.

   Ⓑ I just finished lunch, but I am hungry again.

   Ⓒ I just finished lunch and am hungry again.

   Ⓓ I am hungry again when I just finished lunch.

TOTAL SCORE: ______ /3

Name ____

Weekly Lesson Test
Lesson 9

Oral Reading Fluency

Our solar system used to have nine planets. However, in August 2006, our solar system lost a planet. Pluto is no longer a planet in our solar system. But Pluto did not suddenly disappear from the universe. Pluto is still the same as it ever was, except that its title has changed from "planet" to "dwarf planet."

It may seem like scientists cannot make up their minds. However, change is a natural part of science. Scientific thoughts can change as people learn new things.

What caused scientists to change Pluto's title? Pluto has always been different from the other planets in our solar system. It is smaller than the others. It is even smaller than Earth's moon. It is also more solid, and the shape of its path around the sun is different.

Pluto was discovered in 1930. Since then, scientists have found other objects that are similar to Pluto but not like planets. It made sense to change their thoughts about what Pluto is.

This is how science works. Things can change as scientists learn more. Tomorrow there may be more or fewer planets. Who knows?

______ /WCPM

Name ____

Weekly
Lesson Test
Lesson 10

Selection Comprehension

Choose the best answer for each question.

1. The rangers want to find sea turtle nests MAINLY to
   Ⓐ protect the turtle eggs.
   Ⓑ put tags on baby turtles.
   Ⓒ capture the mother turtle.
   Ⓓ watch the turtle eggs hatch.

2. What happens RIGHT AFTER Emerald makes her nest in the sea grass?
   Ⓕ The rangers see the tag on the turtle.
   Ⓖ Emerald's eggs are taken to a lab to hatch.
   Ⓗ The rangers use flags to mark Emerald's tracks.
   Ⓘ The eggs stay in a lab for nine to eleven months.

3. Which sentence is an OPINION from the selection?
   Ⓐ There are seven species of sea turtles.
   Ⓑ It is named after an American scientist, Richard Kemp.
   Ⓒ She will then cover the hole and return to the sea.
   Ⓓ You have a great attitude, team!

4. Why is Padre Island a special place for sea turtles?
   Ⓕ Rangers work there.
   Ⓖ There is a lot of seaweed.
   Ⓗ Most sea turtles nest there.
   Ⓘ The beach is large and long.

5. Leatherbacks are DIFFERENT from other turtles because they
   Ⓐ have green skin.
   Ⓑ have soft shells.
   Ⓒ are clumsy on land.
   Ⓓ lay nearly 100 eggs.

Name ______________________________

Weekly Lesson Test
Lesson 10

6. What is the main idea of "Emerald's Eggs"?
   Ⓕ Sea turtles need to be protected.
   Ⓖ Rangers need help finding turtle nests.
   Ⓗ Students can learn facts at national parks.
   Ⓘ Turtles have several places in which to lay eggs.

7. The author would MOST LIKELY agree that
   Ⓐ turtles make good pets.
   Ⓑ turtles should be kept in labs.
   Ⓒ newly hatched turtles are cute.
   Ⓓ people should help endangered animals.

8. Green sea turtles have green body fat because they
   Ⓕ can change colors to hide from their enemies.
   Ⓖ absorb the color of water where they swim.
   Ⓗ are coated with slimy green seaweed.
   Ⓘ eat a lot of green-colored algae.

Written Response

9. Suppose you could visit the beach at Padre Island National Seashore. Which kind of turtle would you want to see there? Explain why you would choose that type of turtle. Use details from "Emerald's Eggs" to help support your answer.

____

____

____

TOTAL SCORE: ______ /8 + ______ /2

Name ______________________________

Weekly Lesson Test
Lesson 10

Robust Vocabulary

▶ **Choose the best word to complete each sentence.**

1. I _____ my cousins only when they speak Spanish slowly.
   Ⓐ encircle
   Ⓑ mature
   Ⓒ comprehend
   Ⓓ nurture

2. A mother panda has to _____ a newborn panda for about six months.
   Ⓕ comprehend
   Ⓖ mature
   Ⓗ scan
   Ⓘ nurture

3. The new plastic toy was sturdy yet _____.
   Ⓐ mature
   Ⓑ pliable
   Ⓒ vulnerable
   Ⓓ solitary

4. Houses are often _____ to damage from hurricanes.
   Ⓕ mature
   Ⓖ vulnerable
   Ⓗ solitary
   Ⓘ pliable

5. A polar bear leads a lonely and _____ life.
   Ⓐ solitary
   Ⓑ mature
   Ⓒ exuberant
   Ⓓ vulnerable

Name ______________________________

Weekly Lesson Test
Lesson 10

6. My uncle was able to _____ the map quickly to figure out where we were.

Ⓕ nurture
Ⓖ encircle
Ⓗ scan
Ⓘ infest

7. The pack of wolves was able to _____ their prey before they attacked.

Ⓐ preserve
Ⓑ nurture
Ⓒ infest
Ⓓ encircle

8. An oak tree has to _____ before it will produce acorns.

Ⓕ mature
Ⓖ nurture
Ⓗ scan
Ⓘ comprehend

9. Team members were _____ after winning the state finals.

Ⓐ flexible
Ⓑ pliable
Ⓒ solitary
Ⓓ exuberant

10. The two-ton walrus _____ along on dry land.

Ⓕ scans
Ⓖ lumbers
Ⓗ encircles
Ⓘ infests

TOTAL SCORE: _____ **/10**

Name ______________________________

Weekly Lesson Test
Lesson 11

Selection Comprehension

Choose the best answer for each question.

1. Why did the author write this selection?
   Ⓐ to show how creatures fool each other to survive
   Ⓑ to describe the habits of one special creature
   Ⓒ to warn which creatures are most dangerous
   Ⓓ to explain how a creature catches its food

2. Based on the selection, a deer's markings mostly help it to
   Ⓕ look like trouble
   Ⓖ sneak up on other animals
   Ⓗ blend in with its surroundings
   Ⓘ look different from other animals

3. Why do some animals have markings that make them EASY to see?
   Ⓐ to help them find each other
   Ⓑ to attract prey
   Ⓒ to warn enemies to stay away
   Ⓓ to hide in colorful surroundings

4. How are a snapping turtle and some tropical fish ALIKE?
   Ⓕ Both flash at night.
   Ⓖ Both give off a smell.
   Ⓗ Both have a bad taste.
   Ⓘ Both use a trick to catch food.

5. A polar bear with zebra markings probably would not survive because
   Ⓐ people would be confused.
   Ⓑ the bear could not walk on ice.
   Ⓒ it would be hard to tell it apart from others.
   Ⓓ the bear could be seen in the snow too easily.

Name ___________________________________

6. Why do some birds make sounds like snakes?
   Ⓕ to surprise other birds
   Ⓖ to trick their enemies
   Ⓗ to attract food to eat
   Ⓘ to sing to a mate

7. Birds avoid harmless hornet moths because hornet moths
   Ⓐ are stinging insects.
   Ⓑ cause an upset stomach when eaten.
   Ⓒ have markings like snakes.
   Ⓓ look like stinging insects.

8. How do you know that "Mimicry and Camouflage" is expository nonfiction?
   Ⓕ It has facts and details about a subject.
   Ⓖ It tells the author's personal feelings.
   Ⓗ It has a plot that teaches a lesson.
   Ⓘ It presents events in time order.

Written Response

9. How do camouflage and mimicry help deer and the snapping turtle survive? Use information and details from "Mimicry and Camouflage" to support your answer.

____

____

____

____

____

TOTAL SCORE: ______ /8 + ______ /2

Name ________________________________

Weekly Lesson Test
Lesson 11

Focus Skill: Text Structure: Cause and Effect

▶ **Read the passage. Then choose the best answer for each question.**

The Water Cycle

Have you ever wondered what happens to a puddle after a rainstorm? Some of that water might soak into the ground. The rest of the water in that puddle is about to take a trip through the water cycle.

The first step of the water cycle is evaporation. The sun heats the water in the puddle. As a result, the water turns into a gas. Then this gas, called water vapor, rises into the air.

The next step of the water cycle is condensation. As water vapor floats higher and higher, it gets colder and colder. When it is cold enough, it turns back into drops of water. This is condensation. When many drops of water cling together, they form a cloud.

The final step is precipitation. Eventually, the cloud becomes too heavy for the air to hold, and the water falls back to Earth as rain. Because of precipitation, lakes and oceans get replenished. Much of the rain falls back into puddles, lakes, and oceans. Thus, the water cycle begins again.

1. Which of the following is a cause-and-effect clue word or phrase from the second paragraph?

   Ⓐ if
   Ⓑ since
   Ⓒ then
   Ⓓ as a result

Name ______________________________

Weekly Lesson Test
Lesson 11

2. Which of the following is a cause-and-effect clue word or phrase from the fourth paragraph?
   Ⓕ when
   Ⓖ as a result
   Ⓗ therefore
   Ⓘ Because of

3. Which one of the following states a cause-and-effect relationship?
   Ⓐ The water in the puddle forms a cloud.
   Ⓑ The puddles turn into dirt or pavement.
   Ⓒ The sun's heat turns the water in puddles into water vapor.
   Ⓓ The puddle becomes too heavy for the ground to hold.

4. In the third paragraph, the cause-and-effect clue word *when* comes immediately before
   Ⓕ a cause.
   Ⓖ an effect.
   Ⓗ both.
   Ⓘ neither

TOTAL SCORE: ______ /4

Name ______________________________

Weekly Lesson Test
Lesson 11

Robust Vocabulary

▶ **Choose the word that best completes each sentence.**

1. A dog _____ a wolf, especially in body shape and facial features.
   (A) lumbers
   (B) inspires
   (C) resembles
   (D) lurks

2. You and your family members share many of the same _____.
   (F) intervals
   (G) predators
   (H) traits
   (I) ventures

3. To eat healthfully, _____ foods high in fat.
   (A) avoid
   (B) lure
   (C) mimic
   (D) infest

4. Hayley tried to keep the secret by being _____.
   (F) obvious
   (G) exuberant
   (H) flexible
   (I) deceptive

5. The fisherman tried to _____ the fish.
   (A) avoid
   (B) mimic
   (C) infest
   (D) lure

Name ______________________________

Weekly Lesson Test
Lesson 11

6. The chocolate on Joe's face made it _____ that he had eaten the last piece of cake.
   Ⓕ vulnerable
   Ⓖ obvious
   Ⓗ deceptive
   Ⓘ delicate

7. I tried to _____ a bird by making chirping sounds and flapping my arms.
   Ⓐ encircle
   Ⓑ avoid
   Ⓒ mimic
   Ⓓ scan

8. The mouse did not want to be eaten by the _____.
   Ⓕ traits
   Ⓖ predators
   Ⓗ intervals
   Ⓘ recruits

TOTAL SCORE: _____ /8

Name ____________________

Weekly Lesson Test
Lesson 11

Grammar: Common and Proper Nouns

Choose the best answer for each question.

1. What is the common noun in this sentence?

   Jamal finished his test early.

   Ⓐ Jamal
   Ⓑ finished
   Ⓒ test
   Ⓓ early

2. What is the common noun in this sentence?

   Tigers roam southern India, surviving by hunting.

   Ⓕ Tigers
   Ⓖ roam
   Ⓗ India
   Ⓘ hunting

3. What is the proper noun in this sentence?

   Justine and her brother walked to the library.

   Ⓐ Justine
   Ⓑ brother
   Ⓒ walked
   Ⓓ to

4. What is the proper noun in this sentence?

   Kira collects butterflies and moths.

   Ⓕ Kira
   Ⓖ collects
   Ⓗ butterflies
   Ⓘ moths

TOTAL SCORE: _____ /4

Name ______________________________

Weekly
Lesson Test
Lesson 11

Oral Reading Fluency

It was a bright and sunny June afternoon. Ryan and his family were having a picnic on the freshly mowed field, waiting for the show. The annual Hot Air Balloon Festival was about to begin. Every year, Ryan's family came to participate in this spectacular event.

The first balloon in the sky possessed every color of the rainbow. The next balloon displayed a funny image of a cartoon character. A bright orange-and-yellow sports team logo decorated the third one. Each balloon was unique, and every one was different from the others. The crowd clapped for each balloon as it rose into the summer sky.

As more balloons floated in the air, Ryan had a great idea! While running across the field, he started to take pictures with his new digital camera. He wanted to save these photos so he could look at them anytime he wanted and remember this day forever. Maybe he would even show them to his friends and classmates when school started.

At the end of the show, Ryan had taken more than 40 photographs! He was thrilled with the day's events. He paused and turned around to walk back to find his family. Out of breath and very thirsty, he wondered what could make the day better than it was at this moment. Just then, out of the corner of his eye, he saw a lemonade stand. He smiled and walked over to get a glass of the cold lemony drink.

______ /WCPM

Name ______________________________

Weekly Lesson Test
Lesson 12

Selection Comprehension

Choose the best answer for each question.

1. How do you know that "Mountains" is expository nonfiction?
   Ⓐ It has details about someone's life.
   Ⓑ It has characters and real-life events.
   Ⓒ It tells the author's personal feelings.
   Ⓓ It has facts, photographs, and captions.

2. Why did the author write this selection?
   Ⓕ to explain how mountains form and change
   Ⓖ to tell about an underwater mountain chain
   Ⓗ to describe the world's tallest mountain
   Ⓘ to compare two famous mountains

3. What causes most mountains to form?
   Ⓐ Volcanoes erupt in the ocean.
   Ⓑ Wind blows sand into high piles.
   Ⓒ Large pieces of the earth's crust move.
   Ⓓ Glaciers carry away sheets of granite.

4. What happens when water freezes in cracks in rocks?
   Ⓕ The cracks are sealed.
   Ⓖ The cracks get bigger.
   Ⓗ The rocks get softer.
   Ⓘ The rocks dissolve.

5. What happens when a fault weakens the earth's crust?
   Ⓐ Huge rocks rise or fall.
   Ⓑ Mountains become bare.
   Ⓒ Large glaciers are formed.
   Ⓓ Soil spreads out in a fan shape.

Name ______________________________

6. Which of these would MOST LIKELY be found on a volcanic mountain?

Ⓕ limestone
Ⓖ bare soil
Ⓗ cinders
Ⓘ caves

7. How are dome mountains formed?

Ⓐ They are formed when the earth's crust explodes.
Ⓑ They are formed by underground magma.
Ⓒ They rise from the ocean depths.
Ⓓ They are formed by volcanic eruptions.

8. With which of these sentences would the author MOST LIKELY agree?

Ⓕ Mountain ranges can rise up anywhere.
Ⓖ Mountains can cause changes in weather.
Ⓗ Mountain climbing is a sport most people enjoy.
Ⓘ Mountains on land last longer than those underwater.

Written Response

9. **COMPARING TEXTS** Compare the interview "To the Top of the World" with the selection "Mountains." How are these texts ALIKE? How are they DIFFERENT?

____

____

____

____

____

Name ___________________________

Weekly Lesson Test
Lesson 12

Focus Skill: Text Structure: Cause and Effect

▶ **Read the passage. Then choose the best answer for each question.**

Marco's Bird

One day, Marco's mother came home from work with a surprise for him because he had received good grades in all of his classes. It was a parrot with beautiful green feathers on its wings and royal blue feathers atop its head. The parrot also had a band of red feathers across its chest and bright yellow feathers on the back of its neck. She told Marco to think carefully before he chose a name for his new pet. She told Marco that the name should reflect the bird's personality.

"What would you like to be called?" Marco asked the bird. He spent many hours trying to think of a name for this magnificent bird, but he could not think of one. He thought that his friend Lisa might be better at selecting a name that would be appropriate.

"Marco, I think you should name the bird after me, since we have been friends since first grade," Lisa told him the next day. Marco thought this was a perfect idea. It solved his dilemma, and it would certainly make Lisa happy. That night, Marco made a sign that said "Lisa" and secured it to the bird's cage.

The next day, Lisa came to Marco's house after school. He brought her upstairs to his room where he kept his parrot, and when he opened its birdcage, the parrot suddenly flew over to Lisa and landed on her shoulder. Before Lisa knew what was happening, the bird nipped at her head and pulled the ribbon out of her hair with its curved beak and flew back into its cage. Lisa was very upset. She told Marco that she wished he hadn't named the bird after her after all.

Later, Marco told his mother what had happened.

"A name is very important," she said. "Next time maybe you shouldn't rely on what other people think and trust your own ideas."

Marco already knew the perfect name. "I am going to call her Ribbon," he said.

Name ______________________________

1. Which of the following is a cause-and-effect relationship described in the passage?
   (A) Marco's mother saw a beautiful parrot, so she told Marco to think of a name.
   (B) Marco was thinking of a name, so his mother came home from work.
   (C) Marco's mother brought him a surprise so that Marco could think carefully.
   (D) Marco received good grades, so his mother brought him a surprise.

2. Which of the following is a cause-and-effect clue word or phrase from the first paragraph?
   (F) because
   (G) as a result
   (H) so that
   (I) therefore

3. Which of the following is a cause-and-effect clue word or phrase from the third paragraph?
   (A) when
   (B) because
   (C) since
   (D) then

4. What happens because the parrot pulls the ribbon from Lisa's hair?
   (F) Lisa comes to Marco's house.
   (G) Marco opens the bird's cage.
   (H) Lisa wishes Marco had not named the bird after her.
   (I) Marco secures a sign to the bird's cage.

TOTAL SCORE: ______ /4

Name ___________________________________

Weekly Lesson Test
Lesson 12

Reference Sources

Choose the best answer for each question.

1. What resource would you use to find the world's longest tunnel?
   - (A) an almanac
   - (B) a thesaurus
   - (C) a dictionary
   - (D) a magazine

2. Which of the following would you use to find a synonym for *small*?
   - (F) an almanac
   - (G) a thesaurus
   - (H) a dictionary
   - (I) a magazine

3. Where would you look to find a biography of Franklin Roosevelt?
   - (A) a dictionary
   - (B) a thesaurus
   - (C) an encyclopedia
   - (D) a magazine

4. Where would you look to find the distance between New York and Boston?
   - (F) an atlas
   - (G) a thesaurus
   - (H) a dictionary
   - (I) a magazine

Name ____________________

Weekly Lesson Test
Lesson 12

5. Where would you look to find a news article on a present-day baseball player?
   (A) an almanac
   (B) a thesaurus
   (C) a dictionary
   (D) a magazine

6. Where would you look to find a list of national parks in the United States?
   (F) an almanac
   (G) a thesaurus
   (H) a dictionary
   (I) a magazine

7. Where would you look to find information about volcanoes?
   (A) an almanac
   (B) a thesaurus
   (C) an encyclopedia
   (D) a dictionary

8. Where would you look to find a more interesting word than *happy* to use in your writing?
   (F) an almanac
   (G) a thesaurus
   (H) a dictionary
   (I) a magazine

TOTAL SCORE: ______ /8

Name ______________________________

Weekly Lesson Test
Lesson 12

Robust Vocabulary

▶ **Choose the word that best completes each sentence.**

1. When I smelled smoke, I dialed 9-1-1 for _____ help.
   - (A) constant
   - (B) immediate
   - (C) obvious
   - (D) deceptive

2. The baker _____ added the flour to the cake batter.
   - (F) gradually
   - (G) deceptively
   - (H) constantly
   - (I) obviously

3. The news announcer reported a volcanic _____ in New Zealand.
   - (A) predator
   - (B) depths
   - (C) eruption
   - (D) bond

4. Wood products expand in hot weather and _____ in cold weather.
   - (F) reveal
   - (G) infest
   - (H) avoid
   - (I) contract

Name ______________________

Weekly
Lesson Test
Lesson 12

5. Some animals live in complete darkness in the _____ of the ocean.
   (A) eruption
   (B) depths
   (C) intervals
   (D) bond

6. The answers to the crossword puzzle were _____ in the next edition.
   (F) immediate
   (G) avoided
   (H) constant
   (I) revealed

7. The rain was _____ during the night, resulting in flooding the next morning.
   (A) constant
   (B) immediate
   (C) delicate
   (D) obvious

TOTAL SCORE: _____ /7

Name ______________________________

Weekly Lesson Test
Lesson 12

Grammar: Singular and Plural Nouns

Choose the best answer for each question.

1. Which sentence is written correctly?
   - Ⓐ Ms. Romero is taller than the two other ladies in her office.
   - Ⓑ Ms. Romero is taller than the two other lady in her office.
   - Ⓒ Two man and three woman boarded the airplane.
   - Ⓓ Two mans and three womans boarded the airplane.

2. Which sentence is written correctly?
   - Ⓕ We saw a geese flying overhead.
   - Ⓖ We saw a geeses flying overhead.
   - Ⓗ We saw a goose flying overhead.
   - Ⓘ We saw a gooses flying overhead.

3. Which sentence is written correctly?
   - Ⓐ Mr. Johnson's cow had three calf.
   - Ⓑ Mr. Johnson's cow had three calfs.
   - Ⓒ Wolves looking for food roamed the forest.
   - Ⓓ Wolfs looking for food roamed the forest.

4. Which sentence is written correctly?
   - Ⓕ The team painted the benches by the stadium.
   - Ⓖ The team painted the benchs by the stadium.
   - Ⓗ Three fox hid near the fence.
   - Ⓘ Three foxs hid near the fence.

TOTAL SCORE: ______ /4

Name ____

Weekly Lesson Test
Lesson 12

Oral Reading Fluency

Diamonds are jewels that are considered precious and are often quite expensive, depending upon their size and color. They are also the hardest substances in nature. Diamonds are found in many parts of the world, but the hardest ones are found most often in Australia.

Diamonds have different functions in today's world. People have adorned themselves in jewelry highlighted by diamonds for hundreds of years. The birthstone for the month of April is the diamond. Today, people wear diamonds because they have come to represent enduring love in many cultures. Often an engagement ring has a diamond in its center.

Diamonds are formed deep in the earth. Heat and pressure make them very hard. Volcanic eruptions and shifts in the Earth's crust can push diamonds to the surface. When they are unearthed, diamonds look very different from what you might imagine. They do not look sparkle until they are polished. In fact, people can mistake diamonds for ordinary rocks because they resemble plain rocks in their raw form.

Diamonds appear in different sizes and colors. Each individual diamond's value is measured by its weight. Diamonds also come in a variety of colors from clear to black. Red, blue, and green diamonds are the least common types. These rare diamonds are called fancy diamonds. The most valuable diamonds are pale blue. Diamonds can also come in other hues such as yellow, orange, gray, and brown.

_____ /WCPM

Name ____________________

Weekly Lesson Test
Lesson 13

Selection Comprehension

Choose the best answer for each question.

1. Why does Uncle Paul agree to take Axel down the Salmon River?
   Ⓐ Axel wants to be a forester.
   Ⓑ Axel has just learned to kayak.
   Ⓒ Axel makes a good grade in class.
   Ⓓ Axel hopes to see a forest animal.

2. Why does Axel look for a deep place in the river?
   Ⓕ He thinks he will be safer from the fire there.
   Ⓖ He wants to get water to pour on the fire.
   Ⓗ He wants to do another cannonball dive.
   Ⓘ He is tired of staying close to the shore.

3. Why must the family get off the river?
   Ⓐ River currents are too strong to travel.
   Ⓑ They can't see where they are going.
   Ⓒ Burning trees have fallen across the river.
   Ⓓ Strong winds from the heat blow them back.

4. How does the family escape the fire storm?
   Ⓕ They go over a waterfall to safety.
   Ⓖ They are rescued by the fire warden.
   Ⓗ They move to a burned-out area.
   Ⓘ They paddle faster down the river.

5. Why does Aunt Charlotte tell Axel the legend of the phoenix?
   Ⓐ to help him with his history lessons
   Ⓑ to help him believe that the forest will grow back
   Ⓒ to take his mind off the burned forest
   Ⓓ to get him interested in other wildlife

Name ___________________________

Weekly
Lesson Test
Lesson 13

6. What can readers tell about Uncle Paul?

Ⓕ He thinks clearly even in danger.

Ⓖ He has never been in a fire storm.

Ⓗ He travels on only one river.

Ⓘ He is a strong swimmer.

7. How does the author feel about forest fires?

Ⓐ She wants to prevent all fires.

Ⓑ She is angry because they destroy trees.

Ⓒ She is afraid to go into the forest.

Ⓓ She knows that fires are necessary.

8. How do you know that "Fire Storm" is realistic fiction?

Ⓕ It has events that could not really happen.

Ⓖ It tells about an important person in history.

Ⓗ It has facts and details about the author's life.

Ⓘ It has a character who faces a real-life challenge.

Written Response

9. Why was moving to the burned-out campsite a good decision? Use details and information from "Fire Storm" to explain why.

____

____

____

____

TOTAL SCORE: ______ /8 + ______ /2

Name ____

Weekly Lesson Test
Lesson 13

Focus Skill: Draw Conclusions

▶ **Read the passage. Then choose the best answer for each question.**

The Missing Glasses

Lisette always did her homework assignments after the family had finished their dinner. That night, she helped her father clear the dishes from the dining table, and then she took her textbooks and notebooks out of her backpack. However, when she looked at her worksheet, she did a double take. She couldn't read any of the words! Instead of letters, numbers, and words she saw fuzzy gray markings that didn't resemble anything. She lifted her hands and felt her face only to discover that she was not wearing her glasses.

"Louie!" she exclaimed to her brother. "I don't know where my glasses are, so will you help me look for them, please? I can't do my homework without them!" Louie looked at her and smiled.

"Lisette, trust me, you'll find them soon," he said solemnly, and then he shrugged his shoulders and returned to the kitchen to finish washing the dinner dishes.

Disappointed that Louie wouldn't help, Lisette then rummaged through her book bag, but still came up empty handed. She went into the living room where her grandfather was reading the newspaper. She poked among the books that lined the bookcases but didn't find anything.

"Pepere," she said desperately, "I can't find my glasses anywhere. Will you help me?" He looked up from his paper and smiled at her. Like Louie, he said that he thought she would find her glasses very soon. He then returned his gaze to the newspaper. Lisette could not understand why no one would help her. She went upstairs where her mother was preparing to put the baby to bed. Lisette sighed and leaned wearily against the bedroom doorframe.

Lisette told her mother that she had politely asked Louie and Pepere to help her find her glasses but they only smiled and told her

Name ______________________________

Weekly
Lesson Test
Lesson 13

that she would find them soon enough. "Mom, why won't they help me?" she said.

To Lisette's surprise, her mother looked at her and chuckled softly.

"Lisette," she said, "did you notice that your hair has not been falling in your eyes like it usually does? That is because you'll find your glasses on top of your head!"

1. How does Lisette feel throughout the story?
   (A) amused
   (B) exhausted
   (C) frustrated
   (D) overjoyed

2. What story information did you use to draw this conclusion?
   (F) Lisette leaned wearily against the bedroom doorframe.
   (G) Lisette took papers out of her backpack.
   (H) Lisette always does homework after dinner.
   (I) Lisette helped her father clear the table.

3. What knowledge from real life did you use?
   (A) Family members always want to help when you lose something.
   (B) People feel tired and worn-out when they're frustrated.
   (C) Clearing the table can make a person forget where things have been put.
   (D) People are careless, and they are always losing things.

4. Why did Louie and Pepere refuse to help Lisette search?
   (F) They had chores to do after dinner.
   (G) They were tired after a long day.
   (H) They wanted to finish reading the paper.
   (I) They saw her glasses on her head.

TOTAL SCORE: ______ /4

Name ______________________________

Weekly Lesson Test
Lesson 13

Predict Outcomes

Read the passage. Then choose the best answer for each question.

"I'm scared," said Jada, as she finished her cereal. "I've never been on a school bus. What if it's late, or what if I get sick right there on the bus? How am I going to know where to sit?"

"Everything is going to work out fine," her mother said. "Remember how anxious you were when you were starting first grade and you didn't know anyone? When you got home, you told me that the other students were friendly and started talking to you right away that first day."

"This is different, though," Jada replied.

"Everything new feels so different at first, but you gradually get used to it," said her mother. "Now go on, and show some of that courage I know you have. Your new T-shirt is really cool, but your smiling face and cheerful manner will be even cooler."

While Jada waited for the bus, she thought to herself that once she got to school, she'd be fine. She already knew all of the kids in her class, so it was just the half-hour bus ride that scared her. Her family had always lived near the school, and Jada had walked the two blocks to get there. Jada was not a person who faced changes easily. She liked things that were familiar or stayed the same.

The bus rumbled to a stop in front of Jada's house, arriving right on time. Jada walked up the two huge steps, her eyes on the floor of the bus.

"Good morning to you, Miss Jada," said Ms. Williams, the bus driver. "Sit down next to Lyza, right behind me. She's new on this bus route, too, and she's been saving a seat just for you."

Jada smiled at Lyza.

"Cool T-shirt," said Lyza.

Name ______________________________

Weekly Lesson Test
Lesson 13

1. What do you predict Jada will do next?
   (A) She will get sick.
   (B) She will chose another seat.
   (C) She will become friends with Lyza.
   (D) She will decide to walk to school.

2. Which clue from the story supports your prediction?
   (F) Jada had always walked to school.
   (G) Jada doesn't know where to sit.
   (H) Lyza liked Jada's T-shirt.
   (I) Jada gets sick in cars and on buses.

3. How do you think Jada will feel the next day before getting on the bus?
   (A) playful
   (B) nervous
   (C) calm
   (D) jealous

4. Which clue from the story supports your prediction?
   (F) Jada kept her eyes on the floor of the bus.
   (G) Jada likes things to stay the same.
   (H) Jada likes things better when she's familiar with them.
   (I) Jada wears cool T-shirts.

TOTAL SCORE: ______ /4

Name ______________________________

Weekly Lesson Test
Lesson 13

Robust Vocabulary

Choose the word that best completes each sentence.

1. The driver _____ his route to arrive sooner.
   - Ⓐ discouraged
   - Ⓑ altered
   - Ⓒ scoffed
   - Ⓓ plunged

2. The campers poured water on their _____ campfire.
   - Ⓕ smoldering
   - Ⓖ skeptical
   - Ⓗ discouraged
   - Ⓘ immediate

3. Most people dislike the _____ of washing dishes.
   - Ⓐ plunge
   - Ⓑ depths
   - Ⓒ drudgery
   - Ⓓ eruption

4. The student looked _____ at the skating instructor, who said the jump would be easy.
   - Ⓕ skeptically
   - Ⓖ gradually
   - Ⓗ smolderingly
   - Ⓘ treacherously

Name ______________________________

Weekly Lesson Test

Lesson 13

5. Hikers climbed the steep trail, even though it was slippery and ______.

Ⓐ smoldering

Ⓑ immediate

Ⓒ treacherous

Ⓓ obvious

6. My brother ______ at me when I said that I could build the model in one hour.

Ⓕ altered

Ⓖ revealed

Ⓗ discouraged

Ⓘ scoffed

7. Joshua is often ______ when he does not score a goal during a soccer game.

Ⓐ discouraged

Ⓑ altered

Ⓒ revealed

Ⓓ plunged

8. Do you ______ into your homework after school, or do you put it off until later?

Ⓕ reveal

Ⓖ alter

Ⓗ plunge

Ⓘ scoff

TOTAL SCORE: ______ /8

Name ___________________________________

Weekly Lesson Test
Lesson 13

Grammar: Possessive Nouns

Choose the best answer to each question.

1. Which sentence is correct?

   Ⓐ Jess' sweater is red and gold.

   Ⓑ Jess's sweater is red and gold.

   Ⓒ Mr. Ramos' car needs to be painted.

   Ⓓ Mr. Ramos car needs to be painted.

2. Which sentence is correct?

   Ⓕ The childrens tennis shoes were sparkling white.

   Ⓖ The children tennis shoes were sparkling white.

   Ⓗ The childrens' tennis shoes were sparkling white.

   Ⓘ The children's tennis shoes were sparkling white.

3. Which sentence is correct?

   Ⓐ Tonya decorated the team's lockers.

   Ⓑ Tonya decorated the team lockers.

   Ⓒ Tonya decorated the teams lockers.

   Ⓓ Tonya decorated the teams's lockers.

4. Which sentence is correct?

   Ⓕ Iris's books are on the table.

   Ⓖ Iris' books are on the table.

   Ⓗ Les' jacket is in the closet.

   Ⓘ Les jacket is in the closet.

TOTAL SCORE: ______ /4

Name ____________________

Weekly Lesson Test
Lesson 13

Oral Reading Fluency

Lin awoke early and noticed bright sunlight shining into her room. She loved spending the weekend at her uncle's fishing cabin. Drifting through the open window, the cool air smelled fresh and clean. She inhaled it deeply into her lungs and smiled. A beautiful autumn day was about to begin.

Deciding to go for a hike, Lin dressed warmly and fastened her boots. Storm, her dog, was waiting patiently by the door. Lin always took Storm with her when she went hiking. She stroked the soft hair on the dog's head and when she invited her along, Storm wagged her tail and jumped around excitedly.

Lin's goal was to have an adventure. She hoped to see at least one remarkable thing along her way. The rainbow of leaves that were beginning to fall would certainly be a beautiful sight. Autumn was her favorite time of year!

As Lin and Storm traced their usual path, they paid attention to everything around them. Squirrels were gathering acorns while active birds chirped morning melodies for their forest neighbors. A deer and her fawn nervously watched Lin and Storm near the fallen pine tree.

By the end of their morning journey, Lin was weary and ravenous. When she and Storm reached their front door, a delicious smell greeted them. Lin walked into the kitchen to find Uncle Dave making pancakes. They all ate their fill, and even Storm was rewarded with a few pancakes.

_____ /WCPM

Name ______________________________

Weekly Lesson Test
Lesson 14

Selection Comprehension

Choose the best answer for each question.

1. What happens JUST AFTER Mr. Bailey helps the stranger inside?
   Ⓐ The stranger goes to sleep.
   Ⓑ Mr. Bailey calls the doctor.
   Ⓒ The stranger runs away.
   Ⓓ Everyone has dinner together.

2. How do you know that the stranger is not like everyone else?
   Ⓕ The stranger is confused by buttons.
   Ⓖ The stranger strokes rabbits' ears.
   Ⓗ The stranger blows on hot food.
   Ⓘ The stranger works hard.

3. What makes the stranger seem so mysterious?
   Ⓐ He has a bump on his head.
   Ⓑ He does not talk.
   Ⓒ He wears leather clothes.
   Ⓓ He stares at flying geese.

4. What is the MOST LIKELY reason Mrs. Bailey shivers when they eat soup?
   Ⓕ The stranger's breath is icy cold.
   Ⓖ There is a draft in the house.
   Ⓗ The soup has gotten cold.
   Ⓘ Katy is blowing on the soup.

5. Why does Mr. Bailey think the weather is strange?
   Ⓐ The leaves are starting to change color.
   Ⓑ There is a bit of frost in the air.
   Ⓒ It feels like it is still summer, though it should be fall.
   Ⓓ It is warm in the house.

Name ______________________________________

Weekly Lesson Test
Lesson 14

6. What is the MOST LIKELY reason the stranger cannot take his eyes off the flying geese?
Ⓕ He has a feeling he must move on, too.
Ⓖ He wonders how they stay together.
Ⓗ He wonders when they plan to land.
Ⓘ He has never seen birds look so beautiful.

7. How do you know that "The Stranger" is a fantasy?
Ⓐ The plot teaches a lesson.
Ⓑ Animals seem larger than life.
Ⓒ The main character is not like a real person.
Ⓓ The story tells true events from the past.

8. Why did the author write "The Stranger"?
Ⓕ to give information about the seasons
Ⓖ to persuade readers to visit a farm
Ⓗ to teach what to do after an accident
Ⓘ to entertain readers with a surprising tale

Written Response

9. Explain how you know that the stranger is not like other people. Use details and information from "The Stranger" to help you explain.

____

____

____

____

____

TOTAL SCORE: _____ /8 + _____ /2

Name ______________________________

Focus Skill: Draw Conclusions

Read the passage. Then choose the best answer for each question.

Two Heads are Better than One

Justin had a puzzled look on his face. He was at his desk, working on a drawing. Suddenly he erased it and tried something different. Finally, he stood up, stretched, and yawned.

"I've been working on this idea all weekend," he thought. "Well, I guess that's what it takes sometimes."

Justin was sketching his latest invention. He wanted to build an exciting new toy with wheels and a deck like a skateboard, but he wanted it to be higher off the ground.

"I just need to figure out how to steer this thing," he said to himself.

As he sat back down at his desk, Megan, his sister, knocked on his door.

"There's a rabbit in the backyard," she said. "I think it has a broken leg. Will you help me with it?"

"I think all the animals needing help know where to find you, Megan," Justin teased. "Someday you'll have your own animal hospital."

Together they gathered some small craft sticks, first-aid tape, and some strips of fabric from a sewing project. Megan gently held the rabbit as Justin made a splint for the rabbit's leg. Megan found a cozy box for the rabbit and brought it some lettuce and water.

"Now," Justin said to Megan, "you can help me. I'm working on a new invention, and maybe you can give me some ideas."

They headed back to Justin's room and sat down to look at his drawings together.

Name ______________________________

Weekly
Lesson Test
Lesson 14

1. What conclusion can you draw about Justin from information in the first paragraph?
   - (A) He likes to exercise.
   - (B) He doesn't give up on his ideas.
   - (C) He wants to be an artist.
   - (D) He works every weekend.

2. What conclusion can you draw about Justin from information in the second and third paragraphs?
   - (F) He likes to invent things.
   - (G) He always has problems.
   - (H) He needs to practice skateboarding.
   - (I) He is messy.

3. What conclusion can you draw about Megan from information in the passage?
   - (A) She likes to visit animal hospitals.
   - (B) She often talks to her brother.
   - (C) She keeps rabbits in the backyard.
   - (D) She often helps animals.

4. What conclusion can you draw about Justin and Megan from the last line?
   - (F) They stay home on weekends.
   - (G) They try out Justin's inventions.
   - (H) They get along well together.
   - (I) They look at drawings every day.

TOTAL SCORE: ______ /4

Name ____

Weekly Lesson Test
Lesson 14

Predict Outcomes

▶ **Read the passage. Then choose the best answer for each question.**

Darnell never liked having to make his bed. Tucking in the sheets and folding the bed cover around the pillows seemed like a waste of time. He didn't understand the reason for making a bed. There certainly wasn't anyone in his room looking at his bed when he was at school. On weekends, he would spend a lot of time in his room stretched out his bed, so it got rumpled whether he made it or not. He didn't mind his other chores, but making his bed was one he wished he didn't have to do.

On the other hand, his sister Sharon was always very neat. She insisted on arranging her dolls so that all of them were sitting in the same direction. She washed her dolls' clothes and asked Mom to iron them so they wouldn't have any wrinkles! She was proud that she made her bed every morning. A crease never made its way to Sharon's bed, even when she sat on it, which she rarely did.

"Chairs are for sitting, but beds are for sleeping," she often said.

At breakfast one morning, Darnell was complaining about having to make his bed. Sharon joined in the complaining because it was her turn to take out the trash. Dealing with trash went against her ideas of "neat and clean."

All of a sudden, Darnell and Sharon looked at each other. "Hey, I have an idea!" they said at the same time.

1. What do you predict Darnell will do next?
   - (A) Darnell will take out the trash.
   - (B) Darnell will make his bed.
   - (C) Darnell will dry the dishes.
   - (D) Darnell will refuse to make his bed.

Name ______________________________

Weekly Lesson Test

Lesson 14

2. Which clue from the story supports your prediction?
   Ⓕ Darnell's chore is making his bed.
   Ⓖ Darnell likes drying dishes.
   Ⓗ Darnell doesn't mind doing other chores.
   Ⓘ Darnell can't see the point to making his bed.

3. What do you predict Sharon will do next?
   Ⓐ Sharon will take out the trash.
   Ⓑ Sharon will make Darnell's bed.
   Ⓒ Sharon will wash her dolls' clothes.
   Ⓓ Sharon will learn to iron.

4. Which clue from the story supports your prediction?
   Ⓕ Sharon's chore is taking out the trash.
   Ⓖ Sharon is proud of how she makes beds.
   Ⓗ Sharon enjoys washing her dolls' clothes.
   Ⓘ Sharon's mother usually irons the doll clothes.

TOTAL SCORE: ______ /4

Name ______________________________

Weekly Lesson Test

Lesson 14

Robust Vocabulary

Choose the word that best completes each sentence.

1. Compared to the red paint on the walls, the furniture looked ______.
   (A) trembling
   (B) fascinated
   (C) drab
   (D) treacherous

2. The food seller's cart ______ as the heavy truck rumbled by.
   (F) timid
   (G) peculiar
   (H) fascinated
   (I) trembled

3. Darnell didn't join in the game right away because he is ______ in new situations.
   (A) discouraged
   (B) timid
   (C) drab
   (D) smoldering

4. Eduardo and Chris ______ out the door as the final bell rang.
   (F) dashed
   (G) fascinated
   (H) altered
   (I) scoffed

Name ______________________________

5. A ______ leads a solitary life.
   Ⓐ predator
   Ⓑ hermit
   Ⓒ drudgery
   Ⓓ mimic

6. The ball of yarn ______ our cat Mitten.
   Ⓕ fascinated
   Ⓖ dashed
   Ⓗ altered
   Ⓘ contracted

7. Students in fourth grade ______ have tests, but teachers don't usually schedule them every week.
   Ⓐ gradually
   Ⓑ skeptically
   Ⓒ peculiarly
   Ⓓ occasionally

8. Burnt popcorn has a ______ and unpleasant smell.
   Ⓕ peculiar
   Ⓖ timid
   Ⓗ treacherous
   Ⓘ trembling

TOTAL SCORE: ______ /8

Name ___________________________________

Weekly Lesson Test
Lesson 14

Grammar: Pronouns and Antecedents

Choose the pronoun that best completes each sentence.

1. Maria asked whether _____ could go to the store.
   Ⓐ she
   Ⓑ us
   Ⓒ him
   Ⓓ he

2. Jason had a sweater, but he lost _____.
   Ⓕ him
   Ⓖ he
   Ⓗ it
   Ⓘ her

3. The monkey climbed the tree, and then _____ rested on a branch.
   Ⓐ it
   Ⓑ they
   Ⓒ you
   Ⓓ us

4. The leaves turned gold and red, and then _____ fell.
   Ⓕ it
   Ⓖ he
   Ⓗ you
   Ⓘ they

TOTAL SCORE: _____ /4

Name ______________________________

Weekly Lesson Test
Lesson 14

Oral Reading Fluency

There are many types of dogs that people may choose as pets. The beagle is a very popular choice. Whether beagles are at home or outdoors, they are happy dogs. Beagle owners often describe them as smart and lovable. They get along well with people and make good family pets.

Beagles are easy to recognize. They are small dogs with short hair, long ears, and large brown eyes. The usual colors in their coats are black, tan, and white. Their bodies are close to the ground, but there are two different sizes of the beagle. The smaller one stands less than 13 inches high and weighs about 18 pounds. The larger beagle stands as much as 15 inches high and may weigh up to 30 pounds.

Beagles belong to the group of dogs called hounds. All of the dogs in this group were used as hunting dogs. Many hounds have a keen sense of smell. Beagles are fine hunters because of their excellent sense of smell. They search for animals by keeping their noses to the ground. Stories are told about people in England who kept packs of beagles to use for hunting. In the 1600s, beagles were brought to America, where they helped the settlers hunt small birds and rabbits.

______ /WCPM

Name ______________________________

Weekly Lesson Test
Lesson 15

Selection Comprehension

Choose the best answer for each question.

1. The scouts must pay attention to the Captain because they need to
   - Ⓐ learn how to cook.
   - Ⓑ take turns fishing.
   - Ⓒ try to avoid getting seasick.
   - Ⓓ understand how the ship works.

2. Throughout the selection, Rachel changes by becoming more
   - Ⓕ frightened.
   - Ⓖ grateful.
   - Ⓗ confident.
   - Ⓘ patient.

3. When the Captain calls the scouts "salty sea dogs," she means
   - Ⓐ they are able to snorkel.
   - Ⓑ they know about the ocean.
   - Ⓒ they can swim well in the ocean.
   - Ⓓ they have learned to obey orders.

4. Why are the scouts surprised at Big Munson Key?
   - Ⓕ They thought it would look different.
   - Ⓖ They have to search for driftwood.
   - Ⓗ They have to eat canned rations.
   - Ⓘ They need to build a big fire pit.

5. Why did the author write "The Adventurers"?
   - Ⓐ to teach how to sail a ship
   - Ⓑ to tell about a special sea camp
   - Ⓒ to prove the ocean is fascinating
   - Ⓓ to describe common camping problems

Name ______________________________________

6. Which sentence is a FACT from the selection?
   Ⓕ We aren't landlubbers anymore!
   Ⓖ The ship has been at sea for one week.
   Ⓗ I'm just excited we'll finally get to snorkel!
   Ⓘ Wow, that was incredible!

7. What happens JUST BEFORE Captain Jane and the scouts lower themselves into the water near Big Pine Key?
   Ⓐ Captain Jane reminds everyone not to touch the reef.
   Ⓑ Alicia says she is glad they didn't see any sharks.
   Ⓒ Captain Jane says it is time to head back home.
   Ⓓ The children collect their gear to leave the ship.

8. Which statement by Captain Jane BEST shows that the scouts did a good job on the *Intrepid*?
   Ⓕ It's time to head home.
   Ⓖ There's always more to learn, Alicia.
   Ⓗ You were all so shocked when we first arrived.
   Ⓘ You salty sea dogs will always be welcome!

Written Response

9. Explain why you would or would not like to attend the National High Adventure Sea Base camp. Use details from "The Adventurers" to support your answer.

____

____

____

____

TOTAL SCORE: _______ /8 + _______ /2

Name ______________________________

Weekly Lesson Test
Lesson 15

Robust Vocabulary

Choose the best word to complete the sentence.

1. After the heavy snowfall, the _____ fields sparkled.
   Ⓐ seasoned
   Ⓑ peculiar
   Ⓒ pristine
   Ⓓ fragile

2. Mother says to handle glasses carefully because they are _____.
   Ⓕ fragile
   Ⓖ intrepid
   Ⓗ delectable
   Ⓘ pristine

3. When she chose not to do her homework, Maria lost the _____ of watching television.
   Ⓐ guidance
   Ⓑ drudgery
   Ⓒ eruption
   Ⓓ privilege

4. Our teacher will _____ assign homework over the weekend.
   Ⓕ undoubtedly
   Ⓖ solemnly
   Ⓗ skeptically
   Ⓘ gradually

5. The talented chef prepared a _____ lemon cake.
   Ⓐ seasoned
   Ⓑ delectable
   Ⓒ pristine
   Ⓓ fragile

Name ____________________

6. I watched the crane _____ the steel beam above the highway.
   Ⓕ avoid
   Ⓖ plunge
   Ⓗ cherish
   Ⓘ hoist

7. Mr. Jones asked the salesperson for _____ in selecting a laptop.
   Ⓐ intervals
   Ⓑ guidance
   Ⓒ privilege
   Ⓓ depths

8. A _____ teacher knows ways to make learning fun.
   Ⓕ discouraged
   Ⓖ fragile
   Ⓗ seasoned
   Ⓘ pristine

9. The _____ guide led the climbers out of the Grand Canyon.
   Ⓐ intrepid
   Ⓑ timid
   Ⓒ fragile
   Ⓓ drab

10. I _____ the memories of my grandmother.
   Ⓕ hoist
   Ⓖ contract
   Ⓗ cherish
   Ⓘ avoid

TOTAL SCORE: _____ /10

Name ______________________________

Weekly Lesson Test

Lesson 16

Selection Comprehension

▶ **Choose the best answer for each question.**

1. In the selection, how are most of the inventions the SAME?

Ⓐ They have moving parts.
Ⓑ They fill a need.
Ⓒ They are named for their inventor.
Ⓓ They scare people.

2. The author compares an inventor to a bulldog to show that

Ⓕ an inventor must be fierce.
Ⓖ an inventor must be loyal.
Ⓗ an inventor must be friendly.
Ⓘ an inventor must be determined.

3. How do you know that "So You Want to Be an Inventor?" is expository nonfiction?

Ⓐ It tells a story with a beginning, middle, and end.
Ⓑ It tells the author's personal thoughts and feelings.
Ⓒ It has facts and details about a topic.
Ⓓ It has a first-person point of view.

4. Which sentence is an OPINION from the selection?

Ⓕ "It will never fly!"
Ⓖ They called him "Moon Man."
Ⓗ Even Presidents can be inventors.
Ⓘ Mary Anderson invented windshield wipers.

5. What is the MOST LIKELY reason people laughed at the steamboat?

Ⓐ It went up the Hudson River.
Ⓑ It had a lot of flags.
Ⓒ It looked unusual.
Ⓓ It was really a sawmill.

Name ______________________________

6. Which sentence from the selection states a FACT?
   Ⓕ Wouldn't Henry Ford be amazed at what he had started!
   Ⓖ Your invention might scare people.
   Ⓗ If you want to be an inventor, be a dreamer.
   Ⓘ Garrett Morgan came up with traffic lights.

7. The author wrote "So You Want to Be an Inventor?" to tell about some famous inventors AND to
   Ⓐ persuade readers which invention is the best.
   Ⓑ give advice about becoming an inventor.
   Ⓒ tell a funny story about an inventor.
   Ⓓ describe one special invention.

8. Which would MOST help readers understand the ideas in this selection?
   Ⓕ visiting a museum of famous inventions
   Ⓖ looking at a picture of a famous inventor
   Ⓗ asking whether a friend has invented anything
   Ⓘ reading a mystery about a make-believe invention

Written Response

9. Which invention in the selection do you think has helped people the most? Use details from "So You Want to Be an Inventor?" to support your answer.

____

____

____

____

TOTAL SCORE: ______ /8 + ______ /2

Name ______________________________

Weekly Lesson Test
Lesson 16

Focus Skill: Fact and Opinion

▶ **Read the passage. Then choose the best answer for each question.**

The "Land Down Under"

Australia is both a country and an island. It is located in Earth's southern hemisphere. For that reason, it is often called the "Land Down Under." This large island is the sixth largest country in the world. I think it is one of the most beautiful places in the world.

The geography of Australia varies greatly. Much of the island is flat. Tropical rainforests grow along the eastern coast. Deserts cover much of the central part of the country. The heat in those desert areas is terrible, so large cities are located near the coast. I imagine people must enjoy living near the ocean. Water sports such as surfing and boating are great fun.

Sports are very popular in Australia. People play tennis, golf, soccer, cricket, and rugby. The most interesting game is cricket because it is unique. Playing rugby is dangerous at times.

One of the best attractions in the "Land Down Under" is the Great Barrier Reef. It is the largest coral reef on Earth and stretches over 1,000 miles. People travel from all over the world to see it. The plant and animal life near the reef is amazing.

---

1. Which of the following is a fact from the passage?
   Ⓐ Tropical rainforests grow along the eastern coast.
   Ⓑ I imagine people must enjoy living near the ocean.
   Ⓒ Playing rugby is dangerous at times.
   Ⓓ Deserts cover much of the central part of the country.

Name ______________________________

Weekly
Lesson Test
Lesson 16

2. Which of the following is an opinion clue word from paragraph 1?
Ⓕ think
Ⓖ both
Ⓗ reason
Ⓘ largest

3. Which of the following is an opinion from the passage?
Ⓐ For that reason, it is often called the "Land Down Under."
Ⓑ People play tennis, golf, soccer, cricket, and rugby.
Ⓒ The most interesting game is cricket because it is unique.
Ⓓ This large island is the sixth largest country in the world.

4. Which of these sentences from the passage cannot be proved?
Ⓕ Much of the island is flat.
Ⓖ People travel from all over the world to see it.
Ⓗ The geography of Australia varies greatly.
Ⓘ One of the best attractions in the "Land Down Under" is the Great Barrier Reef.

TOTAL SCORE: ______ /4

Name ______________________________

Weekly
Lesson Test
Lesson 16

Follow Written Directions

▶ **Read the directions for making fruit salad. Then choose the best answer for each question.**

Fruit Salad

Materials

2 oranges, peeled and cut
30 grapes, green or red
2 bananas, sliced
1/4 cup of orange juice
1/4 cup of pineapple juice
wooden spoon
large bowl

Steps to Follow
1. Put the pieces of oranges in the bowl.
2. Add the grapes to the bowl.
3. Add the banana slices.
4. Pour both juices on top of the fruit mixture.
5. Stir the fruit and juice together with the wooden spoon.
6. Let the fruit salad stand for an hour before eating so that flavors blend.

---

1. What is the purpose of these directions?

Ⓐ to explain why fruit and juice are important
Ⓑ to teach readers to follow new recipes
Ⓒ to suggest ways of serving fruit salad
Ⓓ to tell readers how to make fruit salad

Name ______________________________

2. How many kinds of fruit are needed for this recipe?
   (F) two
   (G) three
   (H) six
   (I) thirty

3. To make this fruit salad, what should you do first?
   (A) Put the pieces of oranges in the bowl.
   (B) Add the grapes to the bowl.
   (C) Add the bananas.
   (D) Stir the fruit and juice together with the wooden spoon.

4. Why might the fruit salad taste better an hour after it is made?
   (F) It will have more juice.
   (G) It will be colder.
   (H) The flavors will blend.
   (I) The fruit will get softer.

TOTAL SCORE: ______ /4

Name ______________________________

Robust Vocabulary

Choose the word that best completes each sentence.

1. Even though Mr. Bains is a history teacher, he likes to _____ with car engines in his spare time.
   - Ⓐ perfect
   - Ⓑ tinker
   - Ⓒ forge
   - Ⓓ tremble

2. Even though students played pranks on April Fool's Day, Sam did not want to be a _____.
   - Ⓕ quest
   - Ⓖ barrier
   - Ⓗ hermit
   - Ⓘ hoaxer

3. The _____ garden was littered with ruined flowers.
   - Ⓐ trampled
   - Ⓑ intrepid
   - Ⓒ timid
   - Ⓓ forged

4. Eager to reach the new campsite, the hikers _____ new trails through the wilderness.
   - Ⓕ dashed
   - Ⓖ forged
   - Ⓗ fascinated
   - Ⓘ scoffed

Name ______________________________

Weekly Lesson Test
Lesson 16

5. Juana's goal is to _____ her model airplane by the end of the week.
   (A) tinker
   (B) fascinate
   (C) perfect
   (D) tremble

6. Aiden's _____ to find his lost book took four hours.
   (F) barriers
   (G) hoaxer
   (H) quest
   (I) hermit

7. The _____ that keep the field off limits are constructed of thick ropes.
   (A) quests
   (B) barriers
   (C) hoaxers
   (D) hermits

TOTAL SCORE: _____ /7

Name ______________________________

Weekly Lesson Test
Lesson 16

Grammar: Possessive Pronouns

Choose the best answer for each question.

1. Read this sentence.

   My sister thinks the ring is ______.

   Which of the following words best completes the sentence?

   Ⓐ she
   Ⓑ her
   Ⓒ its
   Ⓓ hers

2. Read this sentence.

   The children made these artworks all by ______.

   Which of the following words best completes the sentence?

   Ⓕ them
   Ⓖ themselves
   Ⓗ theirselves
   Ⓘ himself

3. Read this sentence.

   Kim's bike is red, but ______ is blue.

   Which of the following words best completes the sentence?

   Ⓐ mine's
   Ⓑ my
   Ⓒ mine
   Ⓓ myself

TOTAL SCORE: ______ /3

Name ______________________________

Weekly Lesson Test
Lesson 16

Oral Reading Fluency

Peeking out of his earthen hole, the cautious brown toad studied the yard with his huge round eyes. The rainstorm had stopped, leaving the lawn dotted with puddles. The toad loved splashing in the water. He considered hopping toward a tempting puddle. For the moment, the whole yard belonged only to him.

He cautiously hopped to a mushroom and sat motionless while he considered the puddles nearby. Now that the heavy rain had stopped, hungry insects emerged from their hiding places. Bees buzzed by searching for sweet nectar. Mosquitoes flew around in the damp air hunting for their next meal. The brown toad watched, pondering his next move.

Soon, his stomach growled. He realized what he needed to do next. Greedily eyeing the swift mosquitoes, his favorite meal, he planned his attack. He prepared to snatch one with his long, sticky tongue.

Just as the toad was about to seize his prey, two children ran out of the house. Shouting excitedly, they approached the swing set, which was close to the toad. The toad felt the earth shake from the children's pounding feet. His heart raced. He quickly escaped into his hole, still hungry but grateful to be alive.

_______ /WCPM

Name ______________________________

Weekly Lesson Test
Lesson 17

Selection Comprehension

Choose the best answer for each question.

1. What are the passages in "Just Like Me" MOST LIKE?
   - (A) folktales
   - (B) fantasies
   - (C) tall tales
   - (D) autobiographies

2. What is "Just Like Me" MOSTLY about?
   - (F) how artists see themselves
   - (G) how artists are taught to paint
   - (H) where artists like to paint
   - (I) where artists live today

3. How are most of the artists' pictures the SAME?
   - (A) They are painted with watercolors.
   - (B) They show the artists' feelings.
   - (C) They are painted with colored inks.
   - (D) They show the artists' families.

4. Which sentence written by Mira Reisberg is an OPINION?
   - (F) There's a family portrait on the table.
   - (G) The desert blooms with barely any water.
   - (H) I can't imagine anything more wonderful—other than maybe being a dolphin.
   - (I) My mother and father were Holocaust survivors.

5. What is one way the artists in "Just Like Me" are ALIKE?
   - (A) They all have the same memories.
   - (B) They all use their imagination.
   - (C) They all paint simple shapes.
   - (D) They all like pale colors.

Name ______________________________

6. Based on the selection, where did many of the artists get their ideas for their self-portraits?
   Ⓐ from their childhood experiences
   Ⓑ from their favorite painters
   Ⓒ from their friends
   Ⓓ from their books

7. According to the selection, why are Daryl Wells's four self-portraits all different?
   Ⓕ She wanted the pictures to show how she looked as she grew.
   Ⓖ She used different art materials in each picture.
   Ⓗ She had problems choosing which picture she liked best.
   Ⓘ She did each picture with a different colored crayon.

8. With which sentence would MOST of the artists agree?
   Ⓕ Paint only what you see in real life.
   Ⓖ Copy pictures from books over and over.
   Ⓗ Use bright colors when you paint or draw.
   Ⓘ Let your paintings tell about what you feel.

Written Response

9. What do the artists in the selection have in common? Use details from "Just Like Me" to explain your answer.

____

____

____

____

TOTAL SCORE: ______ /8 + ______ /2

Name ______________________________

Weekly Lesson Test
Lesson 17

Focus Skill: Fact and Opinion

Read the passage. Then choose the best answer for each question.

Jigsaw Puzzles

Have you ever completed a jigsaw puzzle? Chances are that you have. When I was growing up, we had many puzzles in my house; they were the best games I had to play. I loved my school because we had puzzles in the classroom. Puzzles are still a popular form of entertainment and are sold in stores throughout the country.

Jigsaw puzzles come in different shapes and sizes. They got their name from the type of tool, the jigsaw, which was originally used to cut the different pieces. The first puzzles were made from wood, so a strong tool was needed to cut around the curves. Now most of these puzzles are made from paperboard. This material is much lighter, and better for working on puzzles.

The original use of the jigsaw puzzle was for educational purposes. Maps were cut up so that students would have to assemble the puzzle by putting the pieces together in the correct arrangement. People soon realized that putting puzzles together was fun. Before long, popular pictures were put onto jigsaw puzzles for people to put together. The ones with the tiny pieces must have been the most difficult to figure out. They were always hard for me to complete.

The jigsaw puzzle has been around for hundreds of years, and should stay around forever, for a few reasons. One is that it can be used to teach. Another reason is that it is an inexpensive form of entertainment. The fact that it can be used over and over again is a third reason.

Name ______________________________

Weekly Lesson Test
Lesson 17

1. Which of the following is true about opinions?
   Ⓐ They can be proved.
   Ⓑ They are usually correct.
   Ⓒ They are statements of feelings or beliefs.
   Ⓓ They can be checked in most reference sources.

2. Which of the following is a fact from the first paragraph?
   Ⓕ Have you ever completed a jigsaw puzzle?
   Ⓖ They were the best game I had to play.
   Ⓗ I loved my school.
   Ⓘ Puzzles are sold throughout the country.

3. Which of the following is an opinion from the second paragraph?
   Ⓐ Jigsaw puzzles come in different shapes and sizes.
   Ⓑ They got their name from the jigsaw.
   Ⓒ The first puzzles were made from wood.
   Ⓓ Paperboard is better for working on puzzles.

4. Which of the following statements cannot be proved?
   Ⓕ The jigsaw puzzle has been around for hundreds of years.
   Ⓖ The jigsaw puzzle should stay around forever.
   Ⓗ The jigsaw puzzle can be used to teach.
   Ⓘ The jigsaw puzzle can be used over and over again.

TOTAL SCORE: ______ /4

Name ______________________________

Weekly Lesson Test
Lesson 17

Follow Written Directions

▶ **Read the directions for making a party-favor popper. Then choose the best answer for each question.**

> **Party-Favor Poppers**
>
> **Materials**
>
> Safety scissors
> Small cardboard tube
> Wrapping paper
> Ribbon
> Treats such as small toys and stickers
> Tape

Directions:

1. Using safety scissors, cut a zigzag pattern almost all of the way around the middle of a small cardboard tube. Leave $\frac{1}{4}$ inch of the tube uncut.
2. Cut a piece of wrapping paper that is twice as long as the tube and wide enough to wrap around the tube.
3. Place the tube in the middle of the wrapping paper. Roll the wrapping paper around the tube and tape the paper together.
4. Hold the wrapping paper at one end of the tube and twist it to seal it closed.
5. Tie a ribbon around the middle of the twist you just made.
6. Fill the unsealed end of the tube with treats.
7. Twist the paper to close the unsealed end. Then tie a ribbon around it.

Name ______________________________

1. What should you do before you start to make the party-favor poppers?
   Ⓐ Read the directions all the way through.
   Ⓑ Gather the materials.
   Ⓒ Ask questions.
   Ⓓ Read the most important steps twice.

2. Why is step 2 important to the overall project?
   Ⓕ The paper must fit around the popper leaving enough to twist the ends.
   Ⓖ The piece of cut paper can show where the zigzag cut should be.
   Ⓗ There should be enough ribbon to tie around the twisted ends.
   Ⓘ The amount of tape needed depends on how the paper is cut.

3. Why does step 5 need to be done before you can do step 6?
   Ⓐ Tying the ribbon makes the project go faster.
   Ⓑ The ribbon makes the popper look finished.
   Ⓒ The ribbon keeps the end closed so the treats do not fall out.
   Ⓓ Tying the ribbon helps you know how much has been used.

4. Which step should you complete after the tube is filled?
   Ⓕ Four
   Ⓖ Five
   Ⓗ Six
   Ⓘ Seven

TOTAL SCORE: ______ /4

Name ______________________________

Weekly
Lesson Test
Lesson 17

Robust Vocabulary

Choose the word that best completes each sentence.

1. The swans looked ______ as they glided across the pond, gently moving their long, thin necks.
   - Ⓐ seasoned
   - Ⓑ graceful
   - Ⓒ mischievous
   - Ⓓ brilliant

2. Several people told Angela that the tiny, beaded braids in her hair looked ______ and unusual.
   - Ⓕ brilliant
   - Ⓖ barriers
   - Ⓗ graceful
   - Ⓘ exotic

3. Shane never babysat for the Thompsons because their twins were so ______.
   - Ⓐ brilliant
   - Ⓑ exotic
   - Ⓒ mischievous
   - Ⓓ graceful

4. Tim was happy because the teacher wrote "______" across the top of his perfect test paper.
   - Ⓕ exotic
   - Ⓖ brilliant
   - Ⓗ tinker
   - Ⓘ graceful

Name ____________________

Weekly
Lesson Test
Lesson 17

5. All students were asked to ______ in the tug-o-war to add strength to the team.
   Ⓐ tinker
   Ⓑ forge
   Ⓒ participate
   Ⓓ perfect

6. Antonia's ______, who came from Italy, started the restaurant that her grandmother owns.
   Ⓕ hoaxers
   Ⓖ quests
   Ⓗ ancestors
   Ⓘ barriers

TOTAL SCORE: ______ /6

Name ______________________________

Weekly Lesson Test
Lesson 17

Grammar: Subject and Object Pronouns

Choose the best answer for each question.

1. Read this sentence.

Lin and I gave him the information for his report.

Which word is an object pronoun?

Ⓐ Linda
Ⓑ I
Ⓒ him
Ⓓ his

2. Read this sentence.

They called me about my questions.

Which word is a subject pronoun?

Ⓕ They
Ⓖ me
Ⓗ about
Ⓘ my

3. Read this sentence.

Ms. Taylor asked ______ to help load the van.

Which word best completes the sentence?

Ⓐ they
Ⓑ we
Ⓒ I
Ⓓ us

TOTAL SCORE: ______ /3

Name ______________________________

Weekly Lesson Test
Lesson 17

Oral Reading Fluency

Neil Armstrong, an American astronaut, was the first person to walk on the moon. He always wanted to fly, so he took lessons and became a pilot on his sixteenth birthday. He served in the Korean War as a Navy pilot, and his airplane was shot down, but he survived.

Armstrong finished college after the war. Then he worked testing planes and rockets, becoming an astronaut in 1962. In 1966, because the spacecraft Armstrong was flying had technical trouble, he had to land it in the Pacific Ocean.

Armstrong and two other astronauts landed on the moon in 1968. As Armstrong stepped onto the moon's surface, he said, "One small step for man, one giant leap for mankind." When the three men returned to Earth, they visited twenty-one countries around the world, and people thought they were heroes for going to the moon.

After his years as an astronaut ended, Armstrong wanted to share what he knew about space, so he became a college teacher in Ohio. Armstrong has helped the United States space program make plans for future activities. He has helped figure out why some space trips work and others do not. Neil Armstrong has won many awards for his space work.

_______ /WCPM

Name ______________________________

Selection Comprehension

▶ **Choose the best answer for each question.**

1. How do you know that "Hewitt Anderson's Great Big Life" is a fairy tale?

Ⓐ There are real people and events from history.
Ⓑ The events in the story could not happen in real life.
Ⓒ The story is made up mainly of dialogue.
Ⓓ There are animals that act like people.

2. What is Hewitt's MAIN problem in the story?

Ⓕ Hewitt gets trapped in a vat of flour.
Ⓖ Hewitt's parents worry that he is too small.
Ⓗ Hewitt's giant relatives are ashamed of him.
Ⓘ A doctor wants to use Hewitt as his life's work.

3. Why do Hewitt's parents decide to give him survival lessons?

Ⓐ They want him to get used to his big bed.
Ⓑ They are afraid that he will run away.
Ⓒ They want him to be able to live among gigantic things.
Ⓓ They are hoping that the exercise will make him grow.

4. Why does Hewitt like to hear his parents sing?

Ⓕ They sing only when they are happy.
Ⓖ He likes to sing along with them.
Ⓗ He feels comforted by the music.
Ⓘ They teach him the words to the songs.

5. Which action BEST shows that Hewitt can take care of himself?

Ⓐ He rescues his parents when they have problems.
Ⓑ He is able to climb out of a measuring cup.
Ⓒ He likes to solve difficult puzzles.
Ⓓ He rides in his father's pocket.

Name ______________________________

Weekly Lesson Test
Lesson 18

6. How do Hewitt's parents stop worrying?
   Ⓕ They build a room where Hewitt can live safely.
   Ⓖ They decide to give Hewitt more survival lessons.
   Ⓗ They finally find a doctor who can help Hewitt.
   Ⓘ They realize that Hewitt is just the right size.

7. Which sentence BEST tells the theme of the story?
   Ⓐ Don't judge anyone by their size.
   Ⓑ It is fun being small in a big world.
   Ⓒ Giants are really very friendly people.
   Ⓓ Some children grow more slowly than others.

8. Why did the author write this story?
   Ⓕ to describe some unusual golden eggs
   Ⓖ to persuade readers to learn about giants
   Ⓗ to show how hard it is to live in a world of big people
   Ⓘ to entertain with an amusing story about a clever boy

Written Response

9. Explain how you know that Hewitt is a good problem-solver. Use details from "Hewitt Anderson's Great Big Life" to support your answer.

____

____

____

____

____

TOTAL SCORE: ______ /8 + ______ /2

Name ______________________________

Focus Skill: Theme

▶ **Read the passage. Then choose the best answer for each question.**

The New Girl at School

It was Daniela's first day at her new school, and she was nervous about not knowing anyone. To make things worse, she was joining the fourth grade class during the middle of the school year. This was tough because everyone else would already know each other.

At recess, she saw two girls on the swings, so she walked over, smiled, and told them her name. They each said hello and told her their names, Madeline and Lizzy. For a while the three of them played together. Everything seemed fine.

The next day, Daniela saw Madeline in the hall. She found out some terrible news. Madeline told Daniela that Lizzy did not like her and did not want Madeline to play with her either. Daniela was confused because she liked Lizzy, and the news made her sad.

On the bus ride home, Daniela thought about how she should handle her problem. She came up with different ideas. One thought was to be mean to Lizzy since Lizzy did not like her anyway. Another idea was to tell Lizzy that she knew the truth. Finally she decided to do nothing. She thought that just being herself was all she could do anyway.

For the rest of the week, Daniela played with Madeline and Lizzy at recess. All three girls seemed to have fun together each day. Still unsure, Daniela continued with her plan to be herself.

The proof came the next week when Madeline was sick for two days. On both days during recess, Lizzy asked Daniela to play. They had a great time together, and Lizzy even asked Daniela to come to her house after school one day. The change made Daniela very happy. She realized that she had made a good decision to just be herself.

Name ___________________________________

Weekly
Lesson Test
Lesson 18

1. How can you tell that being new will be important to the story?
   Ⓐ The author mentions it in the title and in the first sentence.
   Ⓑ Being new is usually connected to the theme.
   Ⓒ Daniela was starting school in the middle of the year.
   Ⓓ Making friends can be difficult.

2. What was Daniela's main problem?
   Ⓕ Daniela was nervous about being new at school.
   Ⓖ Madeline said that Lizzy did not like Daniela.
   Ⓗ Daniela had to ride the school bus.
   Ⓘ Madeline was sick for two days.

3. What made Daniela realize that she handled her situation the right way?
   Ⓐ Madeline came back to school after two days.
   Ⓑ She solved her problem on the bus ride home.
   Ⓒ She came up with several different ideas.
   Ⓓ Lizzy invited Daniela to her house.

4. What does Daniela learn?
   Ⓕ Making new friends is never easy.
   Ⓖ Keeping up friendships is important.
   Ⓗ People will like you for being yourself.
   Ⓘ Treat others the same way that they treat you.

TOTAL SCORE: ______ /4

Name ______________________________

Weekly Lesson Test
Lesson 18

Narrative Forms

Choose the best answer for each question.

1. Which of the following usually contains gods and goddesses?
   - Ⓐ tall tale
   - Ⓑ pourquoi tale
   - Ⓒ fable
   - Ⓓ myth

2. Which of the following features a larger-than-life main character and is structured in humorous episodes?
   - Ⓕ folktale
   - Ⓖ tall tale
   - Ⓗ fairy tale
   - Ⓘ pourquoi tale

3. Which of the following is usually very short and states a moral at the end?
   - Ⓐ fairy tale
   - Ⓑ fable
   - Ⓒ tall tale
   - Ⓓ myth

4. Which of the following usually has a happy ending and includes make-believe characters?
   - Ⓕ fairy tale
   - Ⓖ folktale
   - Ⓗ myth
   - Ⓘ pourquoi tale

Name ______________________________

Weekly Lesson Test

Lesson 18

5. In which literary form would the ancient character Odysseus sail the seas for 20 years battling different gods and creatures?
   (A) fable
   (B) tall tale
   (C) myth
   (D) pourquoi tale

6. In which literary form might an old man teach a young child about the value of patience?
   (F) fairy tale
   (G) folktale
   (H) myth
   (I) tall tale

7. In which literary form would the Zuni tribe use a coyote and an eagle to explain why the moon and the sun live in the sky?
   (A) pourquoi tale
   (B) myth
   (C) fairy tale
   (D) tall tale

8. In which literary form would Johnny Appleseed journey through the American wilderness planting apple seeds and experiencing many funny situations?
   (F) fable
   (G) tall tale
   (H) pourquoi tale
   (I) myth

TOTAL SCORE: ______ /8

Name ______________________________

Robust Vocabulary

Choose the word that best completes each sentence.

1. The plains seemed _____ and endless as Maria looked west.

   Ⓐ relentless
   Ⓑ resourceful
   Ⓒ vast
   Ⓓ graceful

2. Many kinds of meats, cheeses, fruits, and vegetables made up the _____ supply of food.

   Ⓕ brilliant
   Ⓖ graceful
   Ⓗ bountiful
   Ⓘ resourceful

3. The speaker was a professor of great _____ who was known throughout the country.

   Ⓐ intention
   Ⓑ stature
   Ⓒ barriers
   Ⓓ ancestors

4. Using a rope and two sheets, Sara proved herself _____ by constructing a tent.

   Ⓕ exotic
   Ⓖ bountiful
   Ⓗ resourceful
   Ⓘ vast

Name ______________________________

5. Willie has good _____ to get his work done early, but sometimes he delays doing it.
   Ⓐ intentions
   Ⓑ stature
   Ⓒ ancestors
   Ⓓ barriers

6. The _____ music blasted all night long as Connor tried to sleep.
   Ⓕ vast
   Ⓖ bountiful
   Ⓗ resourceful
   Ⓘ relentless

7. Ray _____ knocked his drink off the table because he was not looking at where he was putting the plate.
   Ⓐ occasionally
   Ⓑ inadvertently
   Ⓒ bountifully
   Ⓓ relentlessly

8. Jill had never cared before, but the emotional speech _____ her to action.
   Ⓕ participated
   Ⓖ roused
   Ⓗ forged
   Ⓘ tinkered

TOTAL SCORE: _____ /8

Name ____________________

Weekly
Lesson Test
Lesson 18

Grammar: Adjectives and Articles

Choose the best answer for each question.

1. Read this sentence.

   Molly's _____ kite flew in the sky

   Which word best completes the sentence?

   Ⓐ this
   Ⓑ colorful
   Ⓒ usually
   Ⓓ the

2. Read this sentence.

   No one is allowed to eat on _____ bus.

   Which word best completes the sentence?

   Ⓕ big
   Ⓖ the
   Ⓗ those
   Ⓘ yellow

3. Read this sentence.

   Joseph is wearing his jacket.

   Where is the best place to put the adjective *blue* in this sentence?

   Ⓐ before *Joseph*
   Ⓑ between *wearing* and *his*
   Ⓒ between *his* and *jacket*
   Ⓓ after *jacket*

TOTAL SCORE: _____ /3

Name ____________________

Weekly Lesson Test

Lesson 18

Oral Reading Fluency

Helping her father make oatmeal raisin cookies was one of Hannah's favorite activities. They had baked them many times before and could do it without even looking at the recipe. Hannah loved the way the house smelled when the cookies were baking.

Hannah's dad asked her to collect all the ingredients they needed while he turned on the oven. As she set the ingredients on the counter, she dropped the eggs. What a mess! Now she had to stop and clean the wasted eggs off the floor.

After cleaning up the mess, she added the ingredients to a large bowl while her dad mixed them together. Then they placed the cookie dough on the prepared cookie sheets. When the oven reached the right temperature for the cookies, Hannah's dad used potholders to put them in the oven to bake.

When the cookies were finished baking and had cooled a bit, Hannah and her dad each sat down with a cookie and a tall glass of milk. Smiling, they bit into their treats, but the cookies tasted bad. Hannah's dad remembered they'd never replaced the broken eggs, and oatmeal cookies don't taste right without all of their ingredients.

______ /WCPM

Name ______________________

Selection Comprehension

Choose the best answer for each question.

1. What does don Arturo bet that he can do?
   (A) that he can make Juan give Araceli the apples
   (B) that he can make Juan tell a lie
   (C) that he can grow better apples than don Ignacio
   (D) that he can make don Ignacio tell a lie

2. Why do don Arturo and his family move into don Ignacio's house?
   (F) The workers need to fix the wall at don Arturo's house.
   (G) Don Arturo wants to speak to Juan Verdades every day.
   (H) Araceli thinks it will help them find a way to win the bet.
   (I) The family knows they will lose the ranch and need a place to stay.

3. How does Juan Verdades feel soon after he gives all the apples to Araceli?
   (A) unhappy
   (B) hopeful
   (C) brave
   (D) proud

4. How do you know that this story is a folktale?
   (F) It has opinions and judgments based on facts.
   (G) It involves animals that act like people.
   (H) It has a plot that teaches a lesson.
   (I) It has information about a topic.

5. Why does Juan Verdades talk to a tree?
   (A) He is practicing telling a lie to don Ignacio.
   (B) He is practicing how he will ask Araceli to marry him.
   (C) He is very lonely and misses talking to someone.
   (D) He is hoping to get the tree to grow more apples.

Name ____________________

6. Why does Juan Verdades promise to give Araceli anything on the ranch?
   Ⓕ He wants her to cook for him.
   Ⓖ He wants to thank her for her kindness.
   Ⓗ He hopes her father will hire him.
   Ⓘ He plans to marry her.

7. What does Araceli MOST LIKELY ask Juan's employer to do?
   Ⓐ help her parents move back to their ranch
   Ⓑ give her father's ranch to Juan Verdades
   Ⓒ allow Juan Verdades to keep his job
   Ⓓ let her keep all the apples that Juan Verdades had picked

8. Why did the author write this story?
   Ⓕ to explain what living on a ranch is like
   Ⓖ to describe a special apple tree on a ranch
   Ⓗ to teach how to solve a challenging riddle
   Ⓘ to teach a lesson about honesty

Written Response

9. **COMPARING TEXTS** How are the fox in "Hard Cheese" and Araceli in "Juan Verdades" ALIKE? Use details from BOTH stories to support your answer.

____

____

____

____

TOTAL SCORE: ______ /8 + ______ /2

Name ______________________________

Weekly Lesson Test
Lesson 19

Focus Skill: Theme

▶ **Read the passage. Then choose the best answer for each question.**

Having Fun

It was our last day together before my grandparents had to return home. I was sad that they would be leaving, and I did not want to waste the day sitting around. Making a memory with them would be a fun way to end our family visit.

The sun was shining, the air was crisp, and the leaves were falling from the trees. I suggested that we visit the huge farm not far from our house, and I was thrilled when everyone agreed! We bundled up in cozy clothes and wore our boots. It had rained, and we knew the fields would be muddy.

When we arrived, we were treated to a surprise. The farmer was giving free hayrides in a wagon drawn by his tractor. Traveling through the fields, we spotted cows, goats, chickens, horses, sheep, and pigs. Cute little baby animals were roaming about, too.

After our ride, we piled into the car. My mom said that we still had an hour before we needed to be at the train station, so Grandpa asked where we might eat lunch along the way. Dad remembered a neat pasta place that was certain to add to our memorable day. We decided to go there for a bite to eat, and while we waited for our meal, the servers sang songs.

Finally heading for the train station, we began to say our good-byes. It was upsetting to see my grandparents leave. I did not want to cry, so I just kept thinking about our great day together. We smiled as we remembered our day at the farm. We laughed while talking about our singing waiter, who sounded terrible. We had a wonderful last day together! Sometimes the best things in life do not have to be planned.

Name ______________________________

Weekly Lesson Test

Lesson 19

1. What is the first clue that tells you having fun will be important to the story?
   Ⓐ The restaurant servers sing and dance.
   Ⓑ The autumn weather is beautiful.
   Ⓒ There is a farm nearby that has animals.
   Ⓓ The word fun is in the title of the story.

2. How do the different settings of the day contribute to the theme?
   Ⓕ They are all within driving distance.
   Ⓖ Everyone seems to enjoy all of the activities.
   Ⓗ The restaurant has good food.
   Ⓘ The train station is a fun place to visit.

3. Which plot event occurs that allows the family to continue their fun together after the visit to the farm?
   Ⓐ Everyone enjoys the hayride in the farm wagon.
   Ⓑ There are cute baby animals roaming in the fields.
   Ⓒ There is time for lunch at a neat place Dad remembered.
   Ⓓ It is finally time to go to the train station.

4. What does the character learn by the end of the story?
   Ⓕ It is not necessary to plan in order to have fun.
   Ⓖ Restaurant servers can sing and dance.
   Ⓗ Grandparents who like to try new things are fun.
   Ⓘ Farms have many different animals.

TOTAL SCORE: ______ /4

Name ______________________________

Weekly Lesson Test
Lesson 19

Narrative Forms

Choose the best answer for each question.

1. Which of the following is true of imaginative literature?
   Ⓐ It is based on stories about real events.
   Ⓑ Characters are based on real people.
   Ⓒ Settings are always real.
   Ⓓ It may contain events that are unrealistic.

2. Which of the following characteristics is true about a fairy tale?
   Ⓕ It states a moral at the end.
   Ⓖ There is only one version of each story.
   Ⓗ It usually has a happy ending.
   Ⓘ Events usually happen in threes.

3. Which of the following characteristics is true of pourquoi tales?
   Ⓐ They explain events in nature.
   Ⓑ They are based on modern science.
   Ⓒ They are untraditional stories.
   Ⓓ They have happy endings.

4. Which kind of story would tell how Pecos Bill cleaned up the western states in America because he was the tidiest cowboy around?
   Ⓕ myth
   Ⓖ tall tale
   Ⓗ fable
   Ⓘ pourquoi tale

Name ______________________________

5. Which kind of story usually ends with a moral?
   (A) fable
   (B) pourquoi tale
   (C) folktale
   (D) tall tale

6. In which kind of story do events often happen in threes?
   (F) pourquoi tale
   (G) folktale
   (H) fairy tale
   (I) myth

7. Which kind of tale would tell about Zeus and the many games that the gods and goddesses played on Mount Olympus?
   (A) myth
   (B) pourquoi tale
   (C) fairy tale
   (D) fable

8. Which kind of story is usually humorous, and features larger-than-life characters?
   (F) fairy tale
   (G) myth
   (H) pourquoi tale
   (I) tall tale

TOTAL SCORE: ______ /8

Name ________________________________

Weekly
Lesson Test
Lesson 19

Robust Vocabulary

Choose the word that best completes each sentence.

1. Students who had been practicing long hours were _____ when their concert was canceled.
   - (A) vast
   - (B) distressed
   - (C) magnificent
   - (D) bountiful

2. After winning first place, the gymnast _____ stood on the stage to receive his medal.
   - (F) relentlessly
   - (G) resourcefully
   - (H) confidently
   - (I) vastly

3. Once the hurricane arrived, the governor _____ a state of emergency.
   - (A) declared
   - (B) insisted
   - (C) gloated
   - (D) roused

4. Grandpa _____ on giving me a second helping of potatoes.
   - (F) gloated
   - (G) roused
   - (H) declared
   - (I) insisted

Name ______________________________

5. The student had not been prepared for the test, so he waited ______ for the results.
   Ⓐ anxiously
   Ⓑ confidently
   Ⓒ resourcefully
   Ⓓ inadvertently

6. When the team ______ by shouting victory cheers at the defeated team, their coach called them poor sports.
   Ⓕ declared
   Ⓖ roused
   Ⓗ gloated
   Ⓘ insisted

7. The artist created a ______ thirty-foot statue of the town's first mayor.
   Ⓐ relentless
   Ⓑ resourceful
   Ⓒ magnificent
   Ⓓ bountiful

TOTAL SCORE: ______ /7

Name ___________________________________

Grammar: Comparing with Adjectives

▶ **Choose the adjective or adjectives that correctly complete each sentence.**

1. My cousin won the prize for growing the _____ watermelon.

Ⓐ more larger
Ⓑ most large
Ⓒ largest
Ⓓ most largest

2. Mr. Fuller's ideas were the _____ of all.

Ⓕ helpfulest
Ⓖ most helpful
Ⓗ most helpfulest
Ⓘ more helpfulest

3. My watch is _____ than Claire's.

Ⓐ shinier
Ⓑ more shinier
Ⓒ shiniest
Ⓓ most shiny

4. Justine did _____ on the spelling test than Adam did.

Ⓕ gooder
Ⓖ better
Ⓗ well
Ⓘ best

TOTAL SCORE: _____ /4

Name ________________________________

Weekly
Lesson Test
Lesson 19

Oral Reading Fluency

A map is a drawing on a flat surface of any part of Earth. Different types of maps show Earth in different ways. Maps often use special pictures or lines to stand for the shape of the land, the height of a mountain, the places where people live, and the roads to travel. People have studied maps for thousands of years.

The maps people made hundreds of years ago were not always correct. For example, in the 1800s people flew in hot air balloons to draw maps. Being above the land gave mapmakers a better view of Earth. From up high they drew what they saw. Today computers help us create the best maps. Computers make maps more exact than hand-drawn maps.

Over ten years ago, government leaders wanted updated maps of the United States. Congress passed the "National Geologic Mapping Act of 1992," which ordered the United States Geologic Survey to make new maps of the country. These maps would provide important information about threats to nature.

Maps are important tools to many people. Pilots use maps to guide them onto airport runways. Students use maps to learn about specific places. Maps help travelers find their way from place to place.

_______ /WCPM

Name ______________________________

Weekly Lesson Test
Lesson 20

Selection Comprehension

▶ **Choose the best answer for each question.**

1. What is the MAIN problem in the selection?

Ⓐ Maggie has a bad cold.
Ⓑ Reggie steps on Agatha.
Ⓒ Lightning is striking near the house.
Ⓓ Maggie's drink cools faster than Noah's.

2. Which word BEST describes Maggie?

Ⓕ curious
Ⓖ grateful
Ⓗ helpless
Ⓘ impatient

3. When Mom points out that the cups are different, she is

Ⓐ giving a hint of what will happen.
Ⓑ using the cups as a symbol.
Ⓒ explaining why the cider is hot.
Ⓓ telling why the cider is so tasty.

4. How do Maggie and Noah solve the mystery?

Ⓕ They collect and study the facts.
Ⓖ They start guessing the answer.
Ⓗ They ask Reggie to help them.
Ⓘ They read a science book.

5. With which statement would the author MOST LIKELY agree?

Ⓐ Anyone can build a robot.
Ⓑ Parrots make the best pets.
Ⓒ Solving mysteries of science can be fun.
Ⓓ Everyone should drink apple cider.

Name ______________________

Weekly
Lesson Test
Lesson 20

6. Which sentence is an OPINION in the selection?
   Ⓕ He is covered with tiny rain droplets.
   Ⓖ I think even robots should be polite.
   Ⓗ My cup is much wider than yours.
   Ⓘ My cider is 95 degrees Fahrenheit.

7. Which action BEST shows that Noah knows a lot about science?
   Ⓐ He notices Maggie's red nose.
   Ⓑ He dries the rain off of Reggie.
   Ⓒ He puts lights into Reggie's eyes.
   Ⓓ He remembers the secret password to get in.

8. What are Maggie and Noah MOST LIKELY to do next?
   Ⓕ Play with Agatha.
   Ⓖ Search for flashlights.
   Ⓗ Make hot apple cider.
   Ⓘ Compare their cider cups.

Written Response

9. How are Maggie and Noah ALIKE? Use details from "The Case of the Too-Hot Cider" to support your answer.

____

____

____

____

TOTAL SCORE: _____ /8 + _____ /2

Name ______________________________

Weekly Lesson Test
Lesson 20

Robust Vocabulary

Choose the word that best completes each sentence.

1. When people praise him, Terry just _____ with pride.
   Ⓐ self-assurance
   Ⓑ ancestors
   Ⓒ beams
   Ⓓ intentions

2. Selina tried to _____ her brother by hiding under the blanket.
   Ⓕ monitor
   Ⓖ confound
   Ⓗ rouse
   Ⓘ declare

3. Tired and _____, Aaron complained about getting soaked in the rainstorm.
   Ⓐ miserable
   Ⓑ gracious
   Ⓒ looming
   Ⓓ ominous

4. Storm clouds were _____, threatening our baseball game.
   Ⓕ looming
   Ⓖ insisting
   Ⓗ gloating
   Ⓘ declaring

5. The weather changed as _____ clouds moved in overhead.
   Ⓐ resourceful
   Ⓑ gracious
   Ⓒ installed
   Ⓓ ominous

Name ______________________________

Weekly
Lesson Test
Lesson 20

6. Renae showed _____ as she walked proudly to accept her prize.
Ⓕ self-assurance
Ⓖ intentions
Ⓗ barriers
Ⓘ beams

7. During the experiment, we had to _____ the changes in the plants and record each change in our journals.
Ⓐ confound
Ⓑ gloat
Ⓒ insist
Ⓓ monitor

8. The hikers suffered from frostbite on their toes because their feet were _____ to cold temperatures.
Ⓕ declared
Ⓖ exposed
Ⓗ installed
Ⓘ insisted

9. Once the new television had been _____ in the family room, the Smiths enjoyed their favorite movies.
Ⓐ distressed
Ⓑ gloated
Ⓒ installed
Ⓓ declared

10. It was very _____ of her to offer my family a place to stay.
Ⓕ ominous
Ⓖ gracious
Ⓗ miserable
Ⓘ relentless

TOTAL SCORE: _____ /10

Name ____________________

Weekly Lesson Test
Lesson 21

Selection Comprehension

Choose the best answer for each question.

1. What is the main problem in "Because of Winn-Dixie"?
   - Ⓐ Winn-Dixie tries to get into the library.
   - Ⓑ Opal has a hard time finding a book.
   - Ⓒ Miss Franny mistakes Winn-Dixie for a bear.
   - Ⓓ Opal has to listen to Miss Franny's story.

2. Why does Miss Franny have the job as librarian?
   - Ⓕ She is the only one who wanted the job.
   - Ⓖ The library was a gift from her father.
   - Ⓗ She knows the answers to everything.
   - Ⓘ Herman W. Block owes her a favor.

3. Why does Miss Franny tell about "mosquitoes so big they could fly away with you"?
   - Ⓐ to show the narrator how rough Florida was
   - Ⓑ to describe the true size of the mosquitoes
   - Ⓒ to make the narrator afraid of mosquitoes
   - Ⓓ to prove that she can handle big animals

4. Based on Miss Franny's story, readers can tell that she
   - Ⓕ is a large and strong person.
   - Ⓖ can act brave even when afraid.
   - Ⓗ has had to deal with bears before.
   - Ⓘ would like to have a bear of her own.

5. Before they become friends, how are Opal and Miss Franny ALIKE?
   - Ⓐ Both have a pet dog.
   - Ⓑ Both are new in town.
   - Ⓒ Both are a little lonely.
   - Ⓓ Both own many books.

Name ____________________________________

Weekly Lesson Test
Lesson 21

6. How do you know that "Because of Winn-Dixie" is realistic fiction?
   Ⓕ The setting could be a real place.
   Ⓖ It has a lesson or moral about life.
   Ⓗ The characters are real people from history.
   Ⓘ It gives information about a different culture.

7. At the end of the selection, why does Miss Franny wink at Opal?
   Ⓐ She agrees that Winn-Dixie should stay by the window.
   Ⓑ She wants Opal to know that they are good friends.
   Ⓒ She thinks that Amanda Wilkinson's book was easy to read.
   Ⓓ She is amused that Amanda Wilkinson is an advanced reader.

8. With which sentence would the author MOST LIKELY agree?
   Ⓕ A library should be a big, fancy place.
   Ⓖ Most dogs should be allowed in libraries.
   Ⓗ All librarians should begin work at a young age.
   Ⓘ Friendships can sometimes be found with unusual people.

Written Response

9. Why would Miss Franny be a good friend? Use details from "Because of Winn-Dixie" to explain your answer.

____

____

____

____

TOTAL SCORE: _____ /8 + _____ /2

Name ______________________________

Weekly Lesson Test
Lesson 21

Focus Skill: Character, Setting, and Plot

Read the passage. Then choose the best answer for each question.

The Surprise

Jordan Brin's mother was a nurse. She worked at the hospital downtown. Jordan usually did her homework and set the dinner table while she waited for her mother to come home from work. As Jordan was getting a snack from the kitchen, she noticed the blinking light on the answering machine.

It was a message from her mother. "Jordan, I have a big surprise for you. Call me when you get home."

The last time her mother had surprised her, the surprise was not what Jordan had expected. Her mother had asked her to help with the annual neighborhood cleanup. Still, Jordan hoped this would be a pleasant surprise. She paged her mom, who called back almost immediately.

"You'll never guess who's here," her mother said gleefully into the phone. "It's Cally Chin."

Jordan had posters of Cally Chin on her bedroom walls. She was a basketball sensation. Jordan's mother explained that Cally had injured herself and had come to the hospital. As Ms. Brin took care of Cally, they became friendly. Now Jordan had a chance to meet Cally in person at the hospital.

Jordan jumped on the first bus headed toward the hospital. It was a great experience. Cally gave Jordan some tips for improving her own basketball skills. She also autographed a basketball for Jordan. This time, her mother's surprise had been great!

Name ______________________________

Weekly
Lesson Test
Lesson 21

1. Who is the main character in the story?
   Ⓐ Jordan Brin
   Ⓑ Jordan's mother
   Ⓒ Cally Chin
   Ⓓ Ms. Brin

2. Which of the following events occurs FIRST in the story?
   Ⓕ Jordan rides a bus to the hospital.
   Ⓖ Jordan talks to her mother on the phone.
   Ⓗ Jordan meets Cally Chin.
   Ⓘ Jordan gets basketball tips from Cally Chin.

3. Where does most of the story take place?
   Ⓐ at Jordan's school and at the hospital
   Ⓑ at Jordan's home and on the bus
   Ⓒ at Jordan's school and at her home
   Ⓓ at Jordan's home and at the hospital

4. Why was Cally Chin at the hospital?
   Ⓕ She was hoping to meet Jordan.
   Ⓖ She was injured.
   Ⓗ She was old friends with Ms. Brin.
   Ⓘ She was very ill.

TOTAL SCORE: ______ /4

Name ________________________________

Robust Vocabulary

▶ **Choose the word that best completes each sentence.**

1. The cake recipe _____ of a few simple ingredients.
   Ⓐ snatched
   Ⓑ consisted
   Ⓒ installed
   Ⓓ exposed

2. The swimmer was _____ after having won four first-place awards.
   Ⓕ select
   Ⓖ miserable
   Ⓗ prideful
   Ⓘ ominous

3. My impatient brother _____ the ball out of my hands.
   Ⓐ snatched
   Ⓑ exposed
   Ⓒ consisted
   Ⓓ installed

4. My grandfather _____ a time when there were no computers.
   Ⓕ intends
   Ⓖ beams
   Ⓗ recalls
   Ⓘ confounds

Name ______________________________

Weekly Lesson Test
Lesson 21

5. Only a _____ group of basketball players will be chosen for the all-city team.
   Ⓐ select
   Ⓑ consisted
   Ⓒ prideful
   Ⓓ miserable

6. In order to learn her lines for the play, Kimberly _____ to practice every evening.
   Ⓕ confounds
   Ⓖ beams
   Ⓗ recalls
   Ⓘ intends

TOTAL SCORE: _____ /6

Name ______________________________

Weekly
Lesson Test
Lesson 21

Grammar: Main and Helping Verbs

Choose the best answer for each question.

1. Read the sentence.

   The two children were playing happily in the sandbox all afternoon.

   Which word is the main verb in the sentence?

   (A) were
   (B) playing
   (C) happily
   (D) afternoon

2. Read the sentence.

   She has been to the zoo before.

   Which word is a helping verb in the sentence?

   (F) has
   (G) been
   (H) to
   (I) before

3. Read the sentence.

   I ______ invited my three best friends to my home.

   Which helping verb best completes the sentence?

   (A) will
   (B) have
   (C) might
   (D) did

TOTAL SCORE: ______ /3

Name ______________________________

Weekly Lesson Test

Lesson 21

Oral Reading Fluency

It had seemed like a dream when Camy's scout troop decided to go camping. However, as she stepped onto the bus, camping began to seem like a nightmare. Looking out the bus window, Camy watched her familiar city blur into strange fields and then mostly trees. Finally, after what seemed like hours, the bus arrived at the park, and the scouts spent the rest of the day arranging the campsite and learning camping rules.

After a long day, the scouts were tucked into their sleeping bags inside their tents. Camy's sleeping bag was itchy, and small rocks poked into her from beneath the tent floor. She heard scary noises that she never heard at home—rustles, clicks, and hoots. She felt like crying, but instead she tried to remember why she had thought camping would be fun.

"Psst . . . Hey, Cam, you sleeping?" It was Camy's tent partner, Vanetta. "Let's look at the stars." The two girls sat side by side in front of their tent and looked up. Camy was amazed at the thousands of stars spread across the night sky, and the sight of them helped her feel calm. After that, Camy felt glad she had come on the camping trip.

_______ /WCPM

Name ____________________

Weekly Lesson Test
Lesson 22

Selection Comprehension

▶ **Choose the best answer for each question.**

1. What is the MAIN problem in the selection?
   (A) Amada's brothers hide her diary.
   (B) Amada's brothers are too noisy.
   (C) Amada misses her best friend.
   (D) Amada must leave her home.

2. Why does Amada write in a diary?
   (F) She has no one to talk to about her plans.
   (G) She needs a way to express her feelings.
   (H) She wants to practice writing in English.
   (I) She is afraid she will forget Juárez.

3. Why does Amada take a rock to California?
   (A) She wants to add it to her collection of unusual rocks.
   (B) She wants to compare it to rocks in the United States.
   (C) The rock reminds her of her home and her best friend.
   (D) She thinks her brothers will like to play with the rock.

4. What does Amada worry about MOST in the story?
   (F) The borrowed car will break down.
   (G) She may never go back to Mexico.
   (H) She will forget how to speak Spanish.
   (I) No one will give them a farewell dinner.

5. Which words BEST describe Amada at the end of the selection?
   (A) proud and strong
   (B) excited and amazed
   (C) anxious and nervous
   (D) lonely and disappointed

Name ______________________________

Weekly
Lesson Test
Lesson 22

6. Which sentence BEST tells the main lesson Amada learns in the story?
   Ⓕ Being away from home makes you feel lonely.
   Ⓖ Writing in a journal is easier than writing a letter.
   Ⓗ You always carry what you really love in your heart.
   Ⓘ Moving to a new place is often an unpleasant experience.

7. What is an important characteristic of a diary?
   Ⓐ It is a personal account of day-to-day events.
   Ⓑ It gives facts and information about a certain topic.
   Ⓒ It has characters that must solve a mystery.
   Ⓓ It exaggerates the strength of a hero.

8. Why is the diary important to Amada and her Nana?
   Ⓕ It helps Amada remember her visit to Nana's house.
   Ⓖ It tells about what happens to Amada every day.
   Ⓗ It is a good place to write facts about Mexico.
   Ⓘ It reminds Amada of Mexico and her culture.

Written Response

9. Explain how Amada changes in the story. Use details from "My Diary from Here to There" to support your answer.

____

____

____

____

TOTAL SCORE: _____ /8 + _____ /2

Name ______________________________

Focus Skill: Character, Setting, and Plot

Read the passage. Then choose the best answer for each question.

The Giant Lobster

Gary had heard about the giant lobster from some friends. It turned out they were right about its size. It weighed thirteen pounds! When he saw it, Gary felt more than awe for this lobster, though. He had read that large lobsters were also old ones. This one was trapped in a tiny tank at the supermarket. The thought of someone eating that poor old guy made Gary very sad.

He wanted to rescue the lobster, but he knew that he had neither the time nor the money to take care of a pet. Besides, where would he put it? Even so, Gary asked the supermarket manager if he would let the lobster go to a good home. The manager explained that lobsters are sold by the pound, and he showed Gary how much the giant lobster cost. The manager could not afford to give away that much money. Then Gary asked his friends to give money to buy the lobster, but his friends were more interested in eating the lobster than saving it.

Finally, Gary called the city zoo. Mr. Hu, an employee of the zoo, said he would try to help. Gary and Mr. Hu worried that someone might buy the lobster before they could save it. Working together, they raised enough money to buy the lobster, and they put it in the children's section of the zoo's aquarium. Mr. Hu put a picture of Gary beside the lobster's new tank.

Name ______________________________

Weekly Lesson Test
Lesson 22

1. How does the supermarket manager affect the events in the story?
   (A) By lowering the price of the lobster, the supermarket manager helps Gary buy the lobster and save it.
   (B) The supermarket manager likes lobsters, so he helps Gary raise money to save the lobster.
   (C) The supermarket manager dislikes Gary's friends; therefore, he will not allow them to buy the lobster.
   (D) Because the supermarket manager is unable to help Gary, Gary must find other ways to save the lobster.

2. Why is Mr. Hu an important character in the story?
   (A) Mr. Hu helps Gary resolve his problem.
   (G) Mr. Hu makes solving the problem in the story more difficult.
   (H) Mr. Hu is the main character in the story.
   (I) Mr. Hu is part of the problem to be resolved in the story.

3. Which is the conflict in the story?
   (A) Gary's friends want to buy the giant lobster, but it is too expensive.
   (B) Gary asks the manager to give the lobster away, but it has been sold.
   (C) Gary wants to save the lobster, but he is unable to buy or keep it.
   (D) Gary's friends want to eat the lobster, but it has been sold.

4. How is the conflict resolved?
   (F) Gary convinces the store manager to give the lobster away.
   (G) Gary's friends buy the giant lobster from the store manager.
   (H) Gary and Mr. Hu worry that someone might buy the lobster.
   (I) Gary and Mr. Hu buy the lobster and put it in the zoo.

TOTAL SCORE: _______ /4

Name ______________________________

Weekly Lesson Test

Lesson 22

Robust Vocabulary

Choose the word that best completes each sentence.

1. My father shaved the beard he wore for five years, and now no one ______ him.

Ⓐ installs
Ⓑ recalls
Ⓒ intends
Ⓓ recognizes

2. Before each play, the team took time to ______.

Ⓕ huddle
Ⓖ burst
Ⓗ select
Ⓘ consist

3. When I was ill, my grandmother came and ______ me.

Ⓐ snatched
Ⓑ intended
Ⓒ comforted
Ⓓ recalled

4. The climb up the steep mountainside and down again was quite a ______.

Ⓕ journey
Ⓖ stature
Ⓗ hoaxer
Ⓘ barrier

Name ______________________________

Weekly Lesson Test
Lesson 22

5. The water balloon was so full that it was about to _____.

Ⓐ huddle
Ⓑ snatch
Ⓒ burst
Ⓓ recall

6. The bulletin board lists many _____ for volunteering in the neighborhood.

Ⓕ ancestors
Ⓖ opportunities
Ⓗ hermits
Ⓘ journeys

TOTAL SCORE: _____/6

Name ___________________________________

Weekly
Lesson Test
Lesson 22

Grammar: Action and Linking Verbs

Choose the best answer for each question.

1. Which of the following sentences contains a linking verb?
   - (A) The choir fell behind in its practice for the show.
   - (B) The squirrel ran into our tree house.
   - (C) The badger was asleep for an hour.
   - (D) The scouts started a campfire.

2. Read this sentence.

   We _____ warmer after we started dancing.

   Which linking verb best completes the sentence?
   - (F) was
   - (G) were
   - (H) is
   - (I) are

3. Read this sentence.

   We _____ our bikes down to the park.

   Which action verb best completes the sentence?
   - (A) rode
   - (B) had
   - (C) wore
   - (D) did

4. Which of the following sentences contains an action verb?
   - (F) She has been discussing her plans all morning.
   - (G) They enjoyed their summer vacation.
   - (H) The group was feeling tired after the trip.
   - (I) Edgar is having friends over tonight.

TOTAL SCORE: _____ /4

Name ______________________________

Weekly Lesson Test
Lesson 22

Oral Reading Fluency

Kids today find it more and more difficult to stay in shape. In past times, young people learned how to search the wilderness for food. They also learned the dances of their culture. Today kids must be more creative to get enough exercise.

You should exercise for at least sixty minutes daily. Your body requires a great deal of energy for this much exercise. Eating a balanced, healthy diet will provide your body with the energy you need to stay in shape. If you have used enough energy by the end of the day, you can even sleep better.

Sixty minutes may seem like a great deal of time to spend exercising, but the time goes quickly when you do something fun. Many students play sports for this reason. Even hide-and-seek can keep your mind entertained and your body in good health. If you exercise alone, you can dance, skate, or ride a bike. Some people like to walk on nature trails, while others take swimming lessons.

Exercise does not have to wear you out to help your body. With practice, you can exercise just enough to make your body feel strong and work well. Even a little exercise every day can improve your health.

_____ /WCPM

Name ______________________

Weekly Lesson Test
Lesson 23

Selection Comprehension

Choose the best answer for each question.

1. What happens AFTER Chester walks in his sleep but BEFORE Mama Bellini opens the newsstand?
   - Ⓐ Chester eats the breakfast Mario brings.
   - Ⓑ Chester is locked in the cricket cage.
   - Ⓒ Tucker offers plans to avoid trouble.
   - Ⓓ Mama throws a magazine at Tucker.

2. Why is the ringing of a bell in the story compared to a fire alarm?
   - Ⓕ Both are loud and sudden.
   - Ⓖ Both tell when to leave.
   - Ⓗ Both make sweet music.
   - Ⓘ Both chime each hour.

3. Why did the author write "The Cricket in Times Square"?
   - Ⓐ to prove that crickets make good pets
   - Ⓑ to teach interesting facts about crickets
   - Ⓒ to explain what mice and cats think about
   - Ⓓ to entertain with a story about animal friends

4. What is the MOST LIKELY reason Tucker and Chester are friends?
   - Ⓕ They both have to work at the newsstand.
   - Ⓖ They are willing to share with each other.
   - Ⓗ They help each other find dropped coins.
   - Ⓘ They both used to live in the same place.

5. Why does the author describe Chester's dream about a storm?
   - Ⓐ to give a hint about what will happen next in the story
   - Ⓑ to tell where and when the story action takes place
   - Ⓒ to describe how a story character looks and acts
   - Ⓓ to explain how the story problem will be solved

Name ____

6. How do you know this story is a fantasy?
   - (F) It gives facts about a topic.
   - (G) The story is written to teach a lesson.
   - (H) The story events could not happen in real life.
   - (I) It takes place at a real time and place in the past.

7. What is the MOST LIKELY reason Tucker gives up his savings?
   - (A) He knows he will feel bad if he doesn't help Chester.
   - (B) Harry points out he will get to keep ninety-three cents.
   - (C) Harry persuades him he can easily find more money.
   - (D) He wants to pay rent for sleeping in the newsstand.

8. Which word BEST describes Chester?
   - (F) foolish
   - (G) honest
   - (H) playful
   - (I) sneaky

Written Response

9. When Chester eats a two-dollar bill, he and Tucker both worry about what will happen. Explain how their ideas for handling the problem are DIFFERENT. Use details from "The Cricket in Times Square" to support your answer.

____

____

____

____

TOTAL SCORE: ______ /8 + ______ /2

Name ______________________________

Weekly Lesson Test
Lesson 23

Focus Skill: Sequence: Story Events

Read the passage. Then choose the best answer for each question.

Parade Day

On the day of the big parade, Ida and Frank woke up early. First, the twins got dressed quickly. Then they began their morning chores around the house. Frank started putting out the cereal for the family's breakfast while Ida set the table. They wanted to make sure that there were no excuses for being late to the parade.

When she got downstairs, Mrs. Re was surprised to see the twins at work. The family finished eating breakfast earlier than usual. Ida and Frank's early work had helped a great deal.

Next, it was time to drive downtown where they would watch the parade. The traffic was heavy, and it was hard to find a parking spot. Finally, they were ready to watch the parade. Ida and Frank had streetside spots and were able to see all the people and floats in the parade without any trouble. As the last float passed the twins, they sighed. They could not wait until next year's parade.

Name ______________________________

Weekly Lesson Test
Lesson 23

1. Which of the following events happens FIRST?
   - Ⓐ Ida and Frank watch the parade.
   - Ⓑ Mrs. Re is surprised to see the twins at work.
   - Ⓒ Ida and Frank start their morning chores.
   - Ⓓ Mrs. Re parks the car downtown.

2. What is Ida doing at the same time that Frank is putting out the cereal?
   - Ⓕ setting the table
   - Ⓖ getting dressed
   - Ⓗ waking up
   - Ⓘ watching the parade

3. What does the family do immediately after breakfast?
   - Ⓐ watch the parade
   - Ⓑ start the morning chores
   - Ⓒ get dressed
   - Ⓓ drive downtown

4. Which word is a signal that the family members have done everything they need to do in order to watch the parade?
   - Ⓕ first
   - Ⓖ then
   - Ⓗ next
   - Ⓘ finally

TOTAL SCORE: ______ /4

Name ____

Weekly Lesson Test
Lesson 23

Use Context Clues

Read the passage. Then choose the best answer for each question.

As we were walking to the park, I realized that we had forgotten our water bottles. It was a steamy day. I knew we would need some water. Therefore, I suggested that we zip home and get the water bottles. My brother countered my idea with the suggestion that we go to the convenience store across the street.

We entered the store. A sign directed us to the back of the store where the chilled drinks were kept. We took out two water bottles and placed them on the checkout counter. Then I remembered that we had brought no money. I was so embarrassed that I felt like racing out of the store! The woman waiting in line behind us told the cashier that she would pay for our water. As the cashier swiped her credit card, he said to us, "You two are pretty lucky."

1. Read this sentence from the passage.

> **Therefore, I suggested we zip home and get the water bottles.**

Which is the best meaning for *zip* as it is used in the passage?

Ⓐ fasten together
Ⓑ go fast
Ⓒ add flavor
Ⓓ carry quickly

Name ___________________________________

Weekly
Lesson Test
Lesson 23

2. Read this sentence from the passage.

My brother countered my idea with the suggestion that we go the convenience store across the street.

Which is the best meaning for *countered* as it is used in the sentence?

Ⓕ put on a table
Ⓖ hit back
Ⓗ answer with another
Ⓘ meet in battle

3. Read this sentence from the passage.

A sign directed us to the back of the store where the chilled drinks were kept.

Which is the best meaning for *chilled* as it is used in the passage?

Ⓐ relaxed
Ⓑ cold
Ⓒ depressed
Ⓓ low

4. Read this sentence from the passage.

As the cashier swiped her credit card, he said to us, "You two are pretty lucky.

Which is the best meaning for *swiped* as it is used in the passage?

Ⓕ hit with a blow
Ⓖ stole
Ⓗ made a sweeping motion
Ⓘ slid quickly through

TOTAL SCORE: ______ /4

Name ___

Weekly Lesson Test
Lesson 23

Robust Vocabulary

Choose the word that best completes each sentence.

1. The ___ doctor worked late into the night to help people injured in the car accident.
   (A) select
   (B) pathetic
   (C) noble
   (D) stingy

2. After her favorite team lost, she walked ___ around the house, not saying a word.
   (F) pridefully
   (G) confidently
   (H) graciously
   (I) forlornly

3. As one of my study goals, I ___ to read for at least one hour every day.
   (A) huddled
   (B) resolved
   (C) comforted
   (D) snatched

4. When my brother gets a new toy, he never wants to share and is always so ___ with it.
   (F) prideful
   (G) noble
   (H) pathetic
   (I) stingy

Name ______________________________

5. I had a strong _____ about how the movie would end.
   Ⓐ opportunity
   Ⓑ suspicion
   Ⓒ stature
   Ⓓ journey

6. We spent hours _____ in the yard before we found my mom's lost ring.
   Ⓕ scrounging
   Ⓖ recognizing
   Ⓗ recalling
   Ⓘ intending

7. When my cousin feels nervous, she will _____ and be unable to sit still.
   Ⓐ huddle
   Ⓑ fidget
   Ⓒ gloat
   Ⓓ recognize

8. The news video of homes damaged in the storm was a _____ sight.
   Ⓕ pathetic
   Ⓖ stingy
   Ⓗ noble
   Ⓘ gracious

TOTAL SCORE: _____ /8

Name ______________________________

Weekly
Lesson Test
Lesson 23

Grammar: Present Tense: Subject-Verb Agreement

Choose the best answer for each question.

1. Read the sentence.

   The spider ______ new thread every time its web is damaged.

   Which verb best completes the sentence?

   (A) had spun
   (B) spun
   (C) spins
   (D) spinning

2. Read the sentence.

   I ______ glad that I get to see you each day after lunch.

   Which verb best completes the sentence?

   (F) was
   (G) were
   (H) had been
   (I) am

3. Read the sentence.

   Rabbits ______ the carrots and greens that they find in the garden each day.

   Which verb best completes the sentence?

   (A) eats
   (B) eating
   (C) were eating
   (D) eat

TOTAL SCORE: ______ /3

Name ______________________________

Weekly
Lesson Test
Lesson 23

Oral Reading Fluency

Jill and her brother Ivan felt very sad. Their family's cat, Shadow, had run away. Shadow had lived with them in their apartment since he was a kitten. The family loved Shadow very much.

When Shadow had been missing for three weeks, Jill and Ivan's mother sat down to talk with them. "It looks like Shadow is not coming back," she said sadly. Jill cried for a long time, but Ivan did not say a word.

When the family went to bed, Ivan did not seem angry, but Jill had never seen him so quiet. Even though Ivan acted differently than she did, Jill knew that he was also very sad. Jill silently promised to help Ivan.

Over the next two weeks, Jill helped Ivan with his chores. While she and Ivan still missed Shadow, Jill noticed that eventually they were able to smile and laugh more easily. One day their mother picked them up from school. "I have a surprise for you," she said. When they got home, there was a tiny kitten sleeping on a towel in a small cardboard box.

"I think we should name him Dexter," Ivan said excitedly. Jill laughed because she knew that name would be perfect.

______ /WCPM

Name ______________________________

Weekly Lesson Test
Lesson 24

Selection Comprehension

Choose the best answer for each question.

1. How do you know that "Mangrove Wilderness" is expository nonfiction?
   Ⓐ It presents events in time order.
   Ⓑ It has facts and details about a subject.
   Ⓒ It has events that could not happen in real life.
   Ⓓ It tells the author's personal thoughts and feelings.

2. What happens to many seedlings AFTER they drop from a mangrove tree?
   Ⓕ They are eaten by the birds.
   Ⓖ They dry up on the hot sand.
   Ⓗ They grow for only one year.
   Ⓘ They drift on water to other places.

3. What is unusual about the way red mangroves grow?
   Ⓐ They can grow in salty water.
   Ⓑ They produce very few seeds.
   Ⓒ They can grow in all climates.
   Ⓓ They are shorter than most trees.

4. What was the author's MAIN purpose for writing "Mangrove Wilderness"?
   Ⓕ to describe the Florida Everglades
   Ⓖ to compare different kinds of trees
   Ⓗ to teach about animals that live in swamps
   Ⓘ to give information about a special kind of tree

5. Which of these is necessary for a red mangrove to grow?
   Ⓐ deep soil
   Ⓑ shallow water
   Ⓒ cool weather
   Ⓓ strong winds

Name ______________________________

6. The mangrove wilderness food chain shows how mangroves
   Ⓕ support animal life.
   Ⓖ develop prop roots.
   Ⓗ become able to resist salt.
   Ⓘ get minerals from water and soil.

7. Under which heading in the selection would readers find information about the height of a mangrove?
   Ⓐ Life Cycle of the Mangrove
   Ⓑ Development of Mangrove Seedlings
   Ⓒ Growth of the Mangrove
   Ⓓ Life in the Mangrove Forest

8. Which would BEST help a reader understand the ideas in this selection?
   Ⓕ looking at pictures of pelicans and herons
   Ⓖ thinking about stories that take place in Florida
   Ⓗ watching a TV program about mangroves
   Ⓘ reading a book written by the same author on another topic

Written Response

9. **COMPARING TEXTS** Explain why the mangrove is "one of the most useful members of the plant kingdom." Use details from BOTH "Mangrove Wilderness" and "Mangrove" to support your answer.

____

____

____

____

TOTAL SCORE: ______ /8 + ______ /2

Name ____

Weekly
Lesson Test
Lesson 24

Focus Skill: Text Structure: Sequence

Read the passage. Then choose the best answer for each question.

Digestion

The body receives energy and nutrients from food. Before this can happen, food has to be broken down into a form that the body can use. The process of breaking down food is called digestion.

Digestion begins in the mouth. During chewing, the teeth break food apart into pieces. The body also produces a liquid in the mouth called saliva that breaks down the sugar in food. After chewing, the food is swallowed. Swallowing pushes food down the throat and into a long tube that leads to the stomach.

Next, the stomach breaks down food into even smaller parts. The stomach produces a liquid that helps break down proteins in the food. The stomach also contracts. This movement mixes the food and the liquid together.

Then food passes into the small intestine, a long, coiled tube. Most of the process of digestion takes place in the small intestine, where food is mixed with different kinds of liquids. These liquids help break down sugars, proteins, and fats.

After food is changed into a form the body can use, it moves into the blood. The inside of the small intestine is lined with very tiny, finger-like blood vessels. Digested food moves into these blood vessels. The blood vessels deliver the digested food to other parts of the body.

Food that is not digested moves into the large intestine. This undigested food is called waste. After passing through the large intestine, wastes leave the body.

Name ___________________________

Weekly Lesson Test
Lesson 24

1. Where does digestion begin?
   (A) in the throat
   (B) in the stomach
   (C) in the small intestine
   (D) in the mouth

2. Where does food go after you swallow it?
   (F) into the stomach
   (G) into the small intestine
   (H) out of the large intestine
   (I) out of the body

3. Where does the blood carry the digested food?
   (A) into the stomach
   (B) into the large intestine
   (C) all over the body
   (D) all over the small intestine

4. What happens to food that is not digested in the small intestine?
   (F) it returns to the small intestine
   (G) it moves into the blood
   (H) it moves into the large intestine
   (I) it returns to the stomach

TOTAL SCORE: ______ /4

Name ______________________________

Use Context Clues

Choose the best answer for each question.

1. Read these sentences.

   Unlike most bees, carpenter bees make holes in wood. That is how they build their nests. The holes these bees bore can damage the wooden parts of a house.

   What does the word *bore* mean in this passage?

   Ⓐ make weary by being dull
   Ⓑ build a nest
   Ⓒ carry from one place to another
   Ⓓ make a hole

2. Read this sentence.

   We were supposed to listen quietly to the speaker, so I had to muffle my laughter when a bird flew into the room.

   What does the word *muffle* mean in this sentence?

   Ⓕ dull the sound of
   Ⓖ share with others
   Ⓗ make louder
   Ⓘ sit in silence

3. Read this sentence.

   The hot flames consumed the dry log that Ben's dad added to the fireplace. Soon the log became a pile of ashes.

   What does the word *consumed* mean in this sentence?

   Ⓐ ignored
   Ⓑ destroyed
   Ⓒ controlled
   Ⓓ leaped

Name ______________________________

Weekly
Lesson Test
Lesson 24

4. Read this sentence.

Unable to read the sign in Spanish, she had a quizzical look on her face.

What does the word *quizzical* mean in this passage?

Ⓕ dazzled
Ⓖ cheerful
Ⓗ puzzled
Ⓘ dreadful

TOTAL SCORE: _______ /4

Name ______________________________

Weekly Lesson Test
Lesson 24

Robust Vocabulary

Choose the word that best completes each sentence.

1. To make fresh lemonade for the picnic, Grandpa will squeeze the lemons to _____ the juice.
   (A) fidget
   (B) extract
   (C) withstand
   (D) resolve

2. Luisa's friends think her dog is _____ because it can ride on a skateboard.
   (F) pathetic
   (G) stealthy
   (H) remarkable
   (I) suitable

3. Our _____ cat silently creeps up on mice.
   (A) stealthy
   (B) suitable
   (C) pathetic
   (D) noble

4. The weather is _____ for swimming, so we will ride our bikes to the pool after lunch.
   (F) pathetic
   (G) stealthy
   (H) suitable
   (I) stingy

Name ______________________________

Weekly Lesson Test
Lesson 24

5. Unable to _____ the freezing weather, the mountain climber turned back before reaching the top.

Ⓐ withstand
Ⓑ extract
Ⓒ huddle
Ⓓ fidget

6. The tall basketball player had a great _____ over the shorter one.

Ⓕ journey
Ⓖ suspicion
Ⓗ ancestor
Ⓘ advantage

TOTAL SCORE: _____ /6

Name ______________________________

Weekly Lesson Test
Lesson 24

Grammar: Past and Future Tense

Choose the correct verb or verbs to complete each sentence.

1. I ______ my hands on the thick towel this morning.
   Ⓐ dried
   Ⓑ dries
   Ⓒ drying
   Ⓓ dryed

2. Stephen ______ his brother on the swing when they go to the park later.
   Ⓕ pushed
   Ⓖ push
   Ⓗ is pushing
   Ⓘ will push

3. Tomorrow I ______ for my turn to talk in class.
   Ⓐ am waiting
   Ⓑ have waited
   Ⓒ would wait
   Ⓓ will wait

4. Last week Hanna ______ the leaves in the schoolyard.
   Ⓕ is raking
   Ⓖ raked
   Ⓗ will rake
   Ⓘ rake

TOTAL SCORE: ______ /4

Name ______________________________

Weekly Lesson Test
Lesson 24

Oral Reading Fluency

Buster was the most unusual dog that Spencer had ever seen in person. He was tall and slender, with a glossy black coat and a tail shaped like a whip. In fact, Buster looked like the dogs pictured in the Egyptian art that Spencer had studied in class.

"What breed of dog is this?" Spencer questioned the man from the dog rescue group.

"He's a greyhound," the man said proudly.

"He's so skinny!" Spencer remarked aloud.

The man laughed along with Spencer's parents. "He may appear skinny to you, but he's actually the ideal weight. Greyhounds are incredible runners, and their bodies should remain very lean and muscular. In fact, Buster used to run in races until he broke his hind leg. Now that he is retired from racing, he requires a good home with a family that will provide him with the love and care that he deserves."

As Spencer approached Buster to pat his back, Buster leaned all of his weight affectionately against Spencer. Buster was big and fast, but he was also friendly. "How could you not love a dog like this?" Spencer thought to himself and smiled.

_______ /WCPM

Name ______________________________

Weekly Lesson Test
Lesson 25

Selection Comprehension

Choose the best answer for each question.

1. The author wrote "Welcome to Chinatown!" MAINLY to
   - Ⓐ describe an unusual festival.
   - Ⓑ teach the history of California.
   - Ⓒ inform about an interesting place.
   - Ⓓ give examples of some special foods.

2. How was Chinatown DIFFERENT after the 1906 earthquake?
   - Ⓕ The buildings looked more like buildings in China.
   - Ⓖ The buildings did not have gates and columns.
   - Ⓗ The buildings had fewer places for restaurants.
   - Ⓘ The buildings looked like the rest of San Francisco.

3. A grocery store in Chinatown is DIFFERENT from most other grocery stores because a store in Chinatown
   - Ⓐ sells fish and seafood.
   - Ⓑ offers many foods from Asia.
   - Ⓒ has newspapers and souvenirs.
   - Ⓓ displays oranges and tangerines.

4. How are "Welcome to Chinatown!" and a travel article ALIKE?
   - Ⓕ Both have characters, setting, and plot.
   - Ⓖ Both describe an interesting city to visit.
   - Ⓗ Both explain how to get around in a city.
   - Ⓘ Both tell different ways to travel to a city.

5. What will "New Destinations" MOST LIKELY talk about next?
   - Ⓐ a special part of Los Angeles
   - Ⓑ the California Gold Rush
   - Ⓒ jasmine rice
   - Ⓓ lion dancers

Name ______________________________

6. Why are people in Chinatown likely to buy many oranges in January?
   Ⓕ That is when oranges are picked.
   Ⓖ The color orange is popular at that time.
   Ⓗ People give the oranges to friends as gifts.
   Ⓘ Oranges are not sold other times of the year.

7. Which sentence is an OPINION from the selection?
   Ⓐ There are Chinatowns in major cities all over the world.
   Ⓑ They built homes, opened restaurants, and started businesses.
   Ⓒ There's always something interesting to see.
   Ⓓ Tea is also served with dim sum.

8. The author believes that Chinatown in San Francisco is
   Ⓕ alarming.
   Ⓖ challenging.
   Ⓗ confusing.
   Ⓘ fascinating.

Written Response

9. What would you most like to see or do if you could go to Chinatown? Explain your choice. Use details from "Welcome to Chinatown!" to support your answer.

____

____

____

____

TOTAL SCORE: _____ /8 + _____ /2

Name ____

Weekly Lesson Test
Lesson 25

Robust Vocabulary

▶ **Choose the best answer for each question.**

1. We could not _____ the house of cards after the fan blew it down.
   - Ⓐ reconstruct
   - Ⓑ fidget
   - Ⓒ symbolize
   - Ⓓ scrounge

2. They decorated the room with balloons to make it look _____.
   - Ⓕ ornate
   - Ⓖ festive
   - Ⓗ pathetic
   - Ⓘ stealthy

3. "This locket will _____ our friendship," Megan said.
   - Ⓐ fidget
   - Ⓑ reconstruct
   - Ⓒ extract
   - Ⓓ symbolize

4. Our outdoor trip was ruined by the _____ of rainy weather.
   - Ⓕ advantage
   - Ⓖ journey
   - Ⓗ misfortune
   - Ⓘ opportunity

5. The bus schedule lists all of the _____ passengers can reach.
   - Ⓐ journeys
   - Ⓑ aspects
   - Ⓒ destinations
   - Ⓓ suspicions

Name ______________________________

Weekly
Lesson Test
Lesson 25

6. The excited audience waited _____ for the show to begin.
   Ⓕ expectantly
   Ⓖ vigorously
   Ⓗ inadvertently
   Ⓘ forlornly

7. The queen's expensive jewels made up the most _____ exhibit at the museum.
   Ⓐ forlorn
   Ⓑ suitable
   Ⓒ stealthy
   Ⓓ ornate

8. The colorful flowers in Mom's garden make it a _____ place to walk.
   Ⓕ pathetic
   Ⓖ gorgeous
   Ⓗ suitable
   Ⓘ stingy

9. Exercising _____ will raise your heart rate.
   Ⓐ expectantly
   Ⓑ vigorously
   Ⓒ confidently
   Ⓓ forlornly

10. Although the movie was slow-paced, certain _____ of it were interesting.
   Ⓕ destinations
   Ⓖ opportunities
   Ⓗ journeys
   Ⓘ aspects

TOTAL SCORE: _____ /10

Name ___________________________

Weekly Lesson Test
Lesson 26

Selection Comprehension

Choose the best answer for each question.

1. Why did the author write "Dragons & Dinosaurs"?
   Ⓐ to explain why dinosaurs disappeared from the earth
   Ⓑ to show where most dinosaur bones have been found
   Ⓒ to entertain with an adventure story about dinosaurs
   Ⓓ to tell how scientists study dinosaurs and draw conclusions

2. How do you know that "Dragons & Dinosaurs" is expository nonfiction?
   Ⓕ It has details about important events in the author's life.
   Ⓖ It tells about events that could not happen in real life.
   Ⓗ It has headings that divide information into sections.
   Ⓘ It tells the author's personal thoughts and feelings.

3. What people of long ago thought were griffins were really
   Ⓐ giants.
   Ⓑ dragons.
   Ⓒ sea monsters.
   Ⓓ extinct animals.

4. What mistake did Richard Owen make?
   Ⓕ He believed that some dinosaurs were reptiles.
   Ⓖ He thought that dinosaurs looked like giant iguanas.
   Ⓗ He thought that all dinosaurs were big and dangerous.
   Ⓘ He believed that dinosaurs should have their own name.

5. What is the main idea of "Dragons & Dinosaurs"?
   Ⓐ Scientists use bones and fossils to understand dinosaurs.
   Ⓑ Scientists have found many dinosaur skulls in the Gobi Desert.
   Ⓒ Many of the first descriptions of dinosaurs were wrong.
   Ⓓ Dinosaurs are interesting creatures that lived long ago.

Name ______________________________

6. Why was the *Apatosaurus* always pictured without a head?
   Ⓕ People thought it was a headless lizard.
   Ⓖ Only the skeleton of the body had been found.
   Ⓗ Its long neck could not support a large head.
   Ⓘ Two scientists argued about what the head looked like.

7. The selection says that *Tyrannosaurus rex* used nearly half its brain to
   Ⓐ see.
   Ⓑ smell.
   Ⓒ feel heat.
   Ⓓ make noise.

8. Based on the selection, computers help scientists understand dinosaurs by
   Ⓕ creating models of how dinosaurs looked and moved.
   Ⓖ identifying the different dinosaur bones that are found.
   Ⓗ showing the color of different types of dinosaurs.
   Ⓘ keeping track of where dinosaur bones are stored.

Written Response

9. Why do scientists studying dinosaur bones have a hard job? Use details and information from "Dragons & Dinosaurs" to support your answer.

____

____

____

____

TOTAL SCORE: ______ /8 + ______ /2

Name ______________________________

Weekly Lesson Test
Lesson 26

Focus Skill: Main Idea and Details

Read the passage. Then choose the best answer for each question.

Your Skin

Did you know that your skin is the largest organ in your body? This amazing organ performs several key functions. Your skin is made up of two main layers. The top layer is waterproof and protects you from germs. The bottom layer is thicker, and contains glands, hairs, and blood vessels.

Your skin helps keep your body at a steady temperature. For example, when you feel hot, sweat glands in the skin produce sweat. This helps your body cool. In addition, blood vessels in the skin widen so that more blood flows into your skin. This allows heat to leave the body more easily. When you feel cold, the blood vessels narrow, and the blood stays deeper inside your body. This keeps your body warm.

Your skin also enables you to feel things. Nerves in your skin sense cold, heat, touch, pressure, and pain. The nerves send information to your brain. In turn, the brain figures out what you are feeling.

Your skin also helps protect you from illness. Skin prevents germs from entering your body. However, germs can enter your body through a cut in the skin. In addition, glands in your skin perform a special job that makes it hard for germs to grow on your skin. Truly, your skin does many important jobs.

1. What is the main idea of paragraph 2?
   (A) Your skin has many important jobs.
   (B) Your skin helps regulate body temperature.
   (C) Your skin keeps germs from entering the body.
   (D) Your skin is the largest organ in the body.

Name ________________________________

2. Which of the following is a detail in paragraph 2 that supports the main idea?

   Ⓕ Sweat glands in the skin help your body cool down.
   Ⓖ Glands in your skin perform a job that helps kill germs.
   Ⓗ Hairs, glands, and other structures make up the skin.
   Ⓘ Nerves in the skin sense cold, heat, touch, pressure, and pain.

3. What is the main idea of paragraph 4?

   Ⓐ Your skin helps keep your body warm.
   Ⓑ Your skin helps you feel cold, heat, and pain.
   Ⓒ Your skin helps keep your body healthy.
   Ⓓ Your skin helps prevent cuts and scrapes.

4. Which of the following is a detail in paragraph 4 that supports the main idea?

   Ⓕ Your skin helps keep you well.
   Ⓖ Blood vessels in the skin can become narrow or wide.
   Ⓗ Skin stops germs from entering your body.
   Ⓘ Your skin is a large organ with many important jobs.

TOTAL SCORE: ______ /4

Name ____________________

Weekly Lesson Test
Lesson 26

Paraphrase

▶ **Choose the best answer for each question.**

1. Read this sentence.

   Some people believe that whole wheat bread is better for the body than white bread because whole wheat contains more fiber.

   Which sentence best paraphrases the sentence above?

   Ⓐ Because it has more fiber, some people think that white bread is better than whole wheat bread.

   Ⓑ White bread tastes better than whole wheat bread because it contains more fiber.

   Ⓒ Because it has more fiber, whole wheat bread may be healthier than white bread.

   Ⓓ Some people believe that white bread is better than whole wheat bread because white bread contains more fiber.

2. Read this sentence.

   Although Smita is a speedy reader, she did not finish the reading assignment on time.

   Which sentence best paraphrases the sentence above?

   Ⓕ Smita easily finished the reading assignment on time because she is such a quick reader.

   Ⓖ Smita finished the reading assignment late because she is a fairly slow reader.

   Ⓗ Smita finished the reading assignment late even though she reads quickly.

   Ⓘ Smita thought she would finish the reading assignment on time because she is a fast reader.

Name ______________________________

Weekly Lesson Test
Lesson 26

3. Read this sentence.

I learned from my dad's photos that moose are large animals with spindly legs, short necks, and enormous antlers.

Which sentence best paraphrases the sentence above?

Ⓐ Moose are large animals with small antlers, short necks, and spindly legs.

Ⓑ My dad's photos of moose show that these small animals have spindly legs, long necks, and gigantic antlers.

Ⓒ According to my dad's photos, moose are large animals with huge antlers, short necks, and long, skinny legs.

Ⓓ My dad's photos show that only large moose have short legs, long necks, and big antlers.

4. Read this sentence.

After ice skating in the park, we went to a small café to get a warm drink.

Which sentence best paraphrases the sentence above?

Ⓕ After spending time at the park, we went to a café.

Ⓖ We went to a café before we went ice skating in the park.

Ⓗ Before going for a warm drink, we ice skated for a long time in the park.

Ⓘ We stopped at a café for a warm drink after we finished skating in the park.

TOTAL SCORE: ______ /4

Name ________________________________

Weekly Lesson Test
Lesson 26

Robust Vocabulary

▶ **Choose the word that best completes each sentence.**

1. The owl hooting in the forest during the night gave the campers an _____ feeling.

Ⓐ aspect
Ⓑ extracted
Ⓒ elegant
Ⓓ eerie

2. After the storm, the fallen trees created many _____ in the road.

Ⓕ aspects
Ⓖ destinations
Ⓗ obstacles
Ⓘ opportunities

3. During the heavy rains, the park by the river was _____.

Ⓐ submerged
Ⓑ complicated
Ⓒ elegant
Ⓓ massive

4. The hikers _____ for hours before finding the trail back to camp.

Ⓕ symbolized
Ⓖ reconstructed
Ⓗ extracted
Ⓘ roamed

Name ______________________________

5. The instructions to assemble the bike were so _____ that we were unable to follow them.
   (A) complicated
   (B) elegant
   (C) submerged
   (D) eerie

6. That _____ dress made of silk and trimmed with pearls is very expensive.
   (F) eerie
   (G) submerged
   (H) elegant
   (I) complicated

7. Weighing as much as 150 tons, the blue whale is a _____ mammal.
   (A) suitable
   (B) massive
   (C) stingy
   (D) festive

8. My grandfather invented a _____ that regularly fills the bird feeder with birdseed.
   (F) suspicion
   (G) misfortune
   (H) destination
   (I) contraption

TOTAL SCORE: _____ /8

Name ___________________________________

Weekly Lesson Test
Lesson 26

Grammar: Irregular Verbs

Read the sentences below. Then choose the verb form that best completes each sentence.

1. I have _____ ten miles so far this year.
   - Ⓐ swam
   - Ⓑ swim
   - Ⓒ swimmed
   - Ⓓ swum

2. The new student _____ a friendly smile all day.
   - Ⓕ wore
   - Ⓖ worn
   - Ⓗ wear
   - Ⓘ weared

3. Our class has _____ a science unit on turtles.
   - Ⓐ began
   - Ⓑ begin
   - Ⓒ beganned
   - Ⓓ begun

4. I have _____ pictures of our pet dog before.
   - Ⓕ drawn
   - Ⓖ drewn
   - Ⓗ drawed
   - Ⓘ drewed

TOTAL SCORE: _____ /4

Name ______________________________

Oral Reading Fluency

Matthew received a notice in the mail. It was printed on computer paper and signed by the school librarian. The notice read, "The following library book is overdue: A Wrinkle in Time. Please return this book to the Windy Hill Elementary School Library as soon as possible. If the book is not returned to the library by Thursday, you will be required to pay for replacing the book."

A lump formed in Matthew's throat. He had known the book was missing for several weeks now, but he had not located it. Matthew searched for the missing book again. He looked in his backpack, he searched every inch of his room, and he even scanned all the titles of the books on the bookshelves.

As Thursday approached, the library book had not turned up. Matthew prepared to ask his parents to lend him the money to pay for the book. He would have to work over the summer to pay his parents back.

Then another notice arrived in the mailbox. Apparently, Matthew had returned the library book—to the city library, not to the school library! The city library had mailed the missing book back to the school library. Finally, the book had been found.

______ /WCPM

Name ______________________________

Weekly Lesson Test
Lesson 27

Selection Comprehension

Choose the best answer for each question.

1. What is the main idea of "Grand Canyon"?
   Ⓐ The Grand Canyon is more than one mile deep.
   Ⓑ The Grand Canyon was formed by the Colorado River.
   Ⓒ People visiting the Grand Canyon stay at campgrounds.
   Ⓓ Visitors to the Grand Canyon learn about the earth's history.

2. How do you know that "Grand Canyon" is nonfiction?
   Ⓕ It has a plot with a beginning, a middle, and an ending.
   Ⓖ It gives facts about places and things that are real.
   Ⓗ It gives details about events in the author's life.
   Ⓘ It has a difficult problem that must be solved.

3. What helped form the sides of the Grand Canyon?
   Ⓐ rockslides
   Ⓑ creeks and streams
   Ⓒ weather and erosion
   Ⓓ trails carved by people

4. What are you MOST LIKELY to see in the deepest part of the Canyon?
   Ⓕ paintings on a boulder
   Ⓖ land covered by a sea
   Ⓗ coyotes and pups
   Ⓘ a predawn storm

5. What is the MOST LIKELY reason the Anasazi Indians built a granary into the Canyon wall?
   Ⓐ They liked the view from the Canyon wall.
   Ⓑ They wanted to keep their food safe from enemies.
   Ⓒ They wanted to paint pictures on the Canyon wall.
   Ⓓ They needed to keep the squirrels away from the food.

Name ______________________________

Weekly Lesson Test
Lesson 27

6. Which sentence from the selection contains an OPINION?
   Ⓕ Thousands of visitors from all over the world have come to view the splendor of the Grand Canyon.
   Ⓖ Pack mules begin a five-hour trip down into the Canyon.
   Ⓗ Clouds of dust follow them as voices from the top fade away.
   Ⓘ The mules continue down the trail to the inner gorge.

7. How is this nonfiction LIKE expository nonfiction?
   Ⓐ Both give facts and information about a subject.
   Ⓑ Both have events that could not really happen.
   Ⓒ Both give details about events in someone's life.
   Ⓓ Both show characters' feelings through dialogue.

8. What can readers tell about the Grand Canyon?
   Ⓕ It has no people living in it.
   Ⓖ It will never get deeper.
   Ⓗ It was formed quickly.
   Ⓘ It is still changing.

Written Response

9. Describe what you would expect to see if you visited the Grand Canyon. Use details from "Grand Canyon: A Trail Through Time" to support your answer.

____

____

____

____

TOTAL SCORE: _____ /8 + _____ /2

Name ______________________________

Weekly Lesson Test
Lesson 27

Focus Skill: Main Idea and Details

Read the passage. Then choose the best answer for each question.

Breathing

What happens when you take a breath? You start a process that delivers oxygen to your entire body. Oxygen travels from your mouth or nose into your lungs. Oxygen moves into tiny blood vessels in your lungs, where through a process called diffusion it passes from the blood vessels to the blood itself. Next, the oxygen-rich blood leaves the lungs. Then it goes to your heart. Blood leaves the heart through a large artery, called the aorta. The aorta takes the blood from your heart to the rest of your body.

After delivering oxygen to all parts of your body, the blood needs more oxygen. Therefore, oxygen-poor blood returns to your heart. Then it goes to your lungs. There, oxygen-poor blood receives more oxygen. The cycle begins again as oxygen-rich blood travels from the lungs, to the heart, and then to the rest of your body. This is how your body gets the oxygen it needs.

1. What is the main idea of paragraph 1?
   - Ⓐ When you take a breath, you bring oxygen into your lungs.
   - Ⓑ Oxygen enters your lungs, and blood carries it to the rest of your body.
   - Ⓒ The lungs have many tiny blood vessels that pick up oxygen.
   - Ⓓ Breathing is one way your body is able to get oxygen from the air.

Name ______________________________

2. Which of the following is a detail in paragraph 1 that supports the main idea?

Ⓕ The aorta takes blood from your heart to the rest of your body.

Ⓖ Oxygen-rich blood goes to the lungs where it receives oxygen.

Ⓗ Blood returns to your heart and then goes to your lungs.

Ⓘ Breathing is a multi-step process for getting oxygen.

3. What is the main idea of paragraph 2?

Ⓐ Oxygen-poor blood picks up oxygen in your lungs.

Ⓑ The blood delivers oxygen to all parts of your body.

Ⓒ Oxygen-rich blood returns to your heart and then to your lungs.

Ⓓ Blood returns to the heart to receive new oxygen and to begin the cycle again.

4. Which of the following is a detail in paragraph 2 that supports the main idea?

Ⓕ Oxygen-rich blood travels through the body.

Ⓖ Blood leaves the heart through the aorta.

Ⓗ Oxygen-poor blood receives oxygen in your lungs.

Ⓘ Taking a breath brings oxygen into your lungs.

TOTAL SCORE: _______ /4

Name ______________________________

Weekly Lesson Test
Lesson 27

Paraphrase

▶ **Read the sentence. Then choose the best answer for each question.**

1. Read this sentence.

   After the soccer match, we rode bikes in the park.

   Which of the following best paraphrases the sentence above?

   Ⓐ After the soccer match, we rode our bikes home.
   Ⓑ We went bike riding during the soccer match.
   Ⓒ Before the soccer match in the park, we went bike riding.
   Ⓓ We went bike riding in the park when the soccer match was over.

2. Read this sentence.

   My mom was grateful that I had helped her carry the groceries, so she fixed a special dessert for me.

   Which of the following best paraphrases the sentence above?

   Ⓕ I was very thankful that my mom carried the groceries, so I made her a special dessert.
   Ⓖ My mom and I ate a special dessert, and then we carried the groceries together.
   Ⓗ My mom thanked me for carrying the groceries by preparing a sweet snack.
   Ⓘ My mom made me carry the food, and then she was grateful that I made dessert.

Name ______________________________

Weekly
Lesson Test
Lesson 27

3. Read this sentence.

Although bats tend to have the same outline in flight, they vary in size.

Which of the following best paraphrases the sentence above?

Ⓐ When flying, bats look alike, and they tend to be about the same size and shape.

Ⓑ Even though bats look alike when they are flying, they differ in size.

Ⓒ Bats are mostly alike in size and flight patterns.

Ⓓ All bats have about the same size and appearance.

4. Read this sentence.

We were certain that our team would win the championship, but it actually lost.

Which of the following best paraphrases the sentence above?

Ⓕ Our team lost the championship even though we expected it to win.

Ⓖ Although we expected it to lose, our team won the championship.

Ⓗ Even though we supported our team, it won the championship.

Ⓘ We were unsure whether our team would win the championship, and it lost.

TOTAL SCORE: ______ /4

Name ___________________________________

Weekly Lesson Test
Lesson 27

Robust Vocabulary

Choose the best word to complete each sentence.

1. In the morning, the dew ______ as the sun shines on the field.
   Ⓐ symbolizes
   Ⓑ reconstructs
   Ⓒ roams
   Ⓓ glistens

2. The scientists dug up objects from the ______ settlement that turned out to be thousands of years old.
   Ⓕ distant
   Ⓖ cascading
   Ⓗ weary
   Ⓘ ancient

3. After three days of hiking, our legs were so ______ that we could barely walk.
   Ⓐ embedded
   Ⓑ weary
   Ⓒ distant
   Ⓓ cascading

4. Rocks are ______ deep in the mud at the bottom of the stream.
   Ⓕ embedded
   Ⓖ roamed
   Ⓗ symbolized
   Ⓘ reconstructed

Name ______________________________

Weekly
Lesson Test
Lesson 27

5. The lion statues on both sides of the bridge look like ______.
   Ⓐ destinations
   Ⓑ sentries
   Ⓒ misfortunes
   Ⓓ contraptions

6. Water from recent floods is washing over the riverbank and ______ the soil.
   Ⓕ symbolizing
   Ⓖ withstanding
   Ⓗ roaming
   Ⓘ eroding

7. As soon as we arrived at the waterfall, we were amazed at the sight of the ______ water.
   Ⓐ scrounging
   Ⓑ ancient
   Ⓒ cascading
   Ⓓ distant

8. The ______ object looked as far away as the mountains.
   Ⓕ distant
   Ⓖ embedded
   Ⓗ submerged
   Ⓘ cascading

TOTAL SCORE: ______ /8

Name ______________________________

Grammar: Contractions and Possessive Nouns

Choose the best answer for each question.

1. Which words make up the contraction *won't*?

Ⓐ *will* and *not*

Ⓑ *were* and *not*

Ⓒ *want* and *not*

Ⓓ *would* and *not*

2. Read this sentence.

My sister ______ like to go to bed at night.

Which of the following best completes the sentence?

Ⓕ doesn't

Ⓖ does'nt

Ⓗ don't

Ⓘ do'nt

3. Read this sentence.

______ cat loves to climb trees.

Which of the following best completes the sentence?

Ⓐ There

Ⓑ They're

Ⓒ Their

Ⓓ They've

4. Read this sentence.

The bus driver asked ______ jacket was left on the bus.

Which of the following best completes the sentence?

Ⓕ whose

Ⓖ who'se

Ⓗ who's

Ⓘ whos

TOTAL SCORE: ______ /4

Name ________________________________

Weekly Lesson Test
Lesson 27

Oral Reading Fluency

Playing outdoors is fun and healthy, but it can also be dangerous to your skin. When you expose your skin to the sun, you risk damage. This can cause skin cancer years later. Skin cancer is the most common form of cancer. It affects about one million people in the United States each year.

Avoid the sun's strongest rays. This is the most important step you can take to protect your skin. The sun's rays are strongest during the middle of the day, even on cloudy days. Clouds screen few of the sun's harmful rays. Therefore, you can damage your skin on a cloudy day without the normal warning signs.

Another step you can take to protect your skin is to cover it. Choose clothing wisely, however. Can you see through the fabric when you hold the garment up to a light? If so, it will not provide much protection from the sun. Dark colors and tight weaves are your best bets. Special protective clothing, including swimsuits, is now available, too. These lightweight, comfortable clothes block many of the sun's rays.

A wide-brimmed hat, sunglasses, and sunscreen are other tools to help protect your skin from the sun. Plan ahead to enjoy sunny days safely.

_______ /WCPM

Name ______________________________

Selection Comprehension

▶ **Choose the best answer for each question.**

1. What is the MAIN reason why the author wrote "The Bunyans"?
   Ⓐ to teach about important United States landmarks
   Ⓑ to explain how to make caves and mountains
   Ⓒ to persuade readers that the Bunyans were real people
   Ⓓ to entertain with an amusing story

2. Why did the author write "The lumberjack pulled up an acre of dry cane and fashioned a torch . . ."?
   Ⓕ to show how cane was used in the past
   Ⓖ to show how Paul Bunyan lit his home
   Ⓗ to show that everything about Paul Bunyan is very large
   Ⓘ to show that torches were made differently in those days

3. How do you know that "The Bunyans" is a tall tale?
   Ⓐ It has a plot with a beginning, a middle, and an ending.
   Ⓑ It has humor, folk heroes, and impossible happenings.
   Ⓒ It has real people, places, and events from the past.
   Ⓓ It has the author's personal thoughts and feelings.

4. How did Ma and Pa Bunyan get the bears out of Teeny's hair?
   Ⓕ They put her under a huge waterfall.
   Ⓖ They washed the bears out in the sink.
   Ⓗ They used a big comb to pull them out.
   Ⓘ They used hot water and a lot of soap.

5. What is the main idea of "The Bunyans"?
   Ⓐ Paul Bunyan and his wife created a huge crystal cave.
   Ⓑ Some familiar landmarks were made by the Bunyans.
   Ⓒ Paul Bunyan and his wife had two very large children.
   Ⓓ The Bunyans were a family of large people living in Maine.

Name ______________________________

6. Why does the author write that Paul Bunyan's grin was "as wide as the Missouri River"?
   Ⓕ to show that Paul Bunyan is very happy
   Ⓖ to prove that Paul Bunyan has traveled
   Ⓗ to show that Paul Bunyan is from Missouri
   Ⓘ to explain that Paul Bunyan looks strange

7. Why did the Bunyans like to go camping in Wyoming?
   Ⓐ Teeny liked to sleep outdoors.
   Ⓑ Little Jean liked to carve the rocks.
   Ⓒ They could wash their clothes in hot water.
   Ⓓ They thought the mountains were beautiful.

8. Which word BEST describes Little Jean?
   Ⓕ sad
   Ⓖ curious
   Ⓗ proud
   Ⓘ shy

READ THINK EXPLAIN

Written Response

9. In what ways does Ma Bunyan seem like a real person? Use details from "The Bunyans" to support your answer.

____

____

____

____

TOTAL SCORE: ______ /8 + ______ /2

Name ______________________________

Weekly Lesson Test
Lesson 28

Focus Skill: Figurative Language

Read the passage. Then choose the best answer for each question.

The New Puppy

Izumi was watching a bird sing as she opened the wooden gate to her cousin's backyard. Just then, a fluffy little puppy shot out of the backyard like a racehorse at its starting gate. It was an accident waiting to happen. Izumi's heart thumped loudly in her chest. What was happening? Was that her new puppy? She turned and stared. The puppy looked like a cotton ball blowing down the street.

"Go get it! Hurry!" Izumi's cousin Yoko yelled at her.

Izumi started running after the puppy. It looked like a speck that was a million miles away. Izumi kept running. She was breathing heavily now. However, she kept chasing the bouncing white speck in the distance. Suddenly she could not see it anymore.

She stopped where she thought she had lost sight of the puppy. She searched all the places where the puppy could have gone. Then she saw it. It was curled into a ball under a hedge, sleeping like a baby. A leafy bush hugged the little puppy as the puppy slept peacefully in its arms.

Izumi gently picked up the puppy and held it close. She sniffed its tiny neck and muzzle. The scent of a puppy was like perfume to her nose. Finally, she had a puppy of her own, and it was a gem!

1. Which type of figurative language compares the puppy to a cotton ball in paragraph 1?

   Ⓐ idiom
   Ⓑ simile
   Ⓒ metaphor
   Ⓓ personification

Name ______________________________

Weekly Lesson Test
Lesson 28

2. In paragraph 2, the author says that the puppy was "a million miles away." This is an example of which type of figurative language?
   - Ⓕ metaphor
   - Ⓖ personification
   - Ⓗ hyperbole
   - Ⓘ idiom

3. Which of the following is an example of an idiom?
   - Ⓐ like a racehorse at its starting gate
   - Ⓑ an accident waiting to happen
   - Ⓒ like perfume to her nose
   - Ⓓ a bouncing white speck in the distance

4. In paragraph 3, the author says, "A leafy bush hugged the little puppy." This is an example of which type of figurative language?
   - Ⓕ metaphor
   - Ⓖ hyperbole
   - Ⓗ idiom
   - Ⓘ personification

TOTAL SCORE: ______ /4

Name ________________________________

Robust Vocabulary

Choose the best word to complete each sentence.

1. The ship that carried hundreds of passengers was ______ compared with the smaller ships we had seen.
   Ⓐ hearty
   Ⓑ colossal
   Ⓒ fanciful
   Ⓓ ancient

2. Janelle used her imagination to draw a ______ picture of a make-believe land.
   Ⓕ colossal
   Ⓖ fanciful
   Ⓗ behemoth
   Ⓘ hearty

3. The friendly king ______ greeted his honored guests.
   Ⓐ cordially
   Ⓑ massively
   Ⓒ ornately
   Ⓓ forlornly

4. Making the rabbit disappear into a hat was an ______, but the children thought that the rabbit had truly vanished.
   Ⓕ opportunity
   Ⓖ obstacle
   Ⓗ illusion
   Ⓘ advantage

Name ______________________________

Weekly Lesson Test
Lesson 28

5. The dinosaurs must have left ______ footprints when they walked due to their great size.
   Ⓐ festive
   Ⓑ scenic
   Ⓒ fanciful
   Ⓓ behemoth

6. We enjoyed the ______ view of the countryside from the tower.
   Ⓕ colossal
   Ⓖ behemoth
   Ⓗ fanciful
   Ⓘ scenic

7. My grandmother's vegetable soup is so ______ that it is a meal by itself.
   Ⓐ behemoth
   Ⓑ scenic
   Ⓒ hearty
   Ⓓ weary

TOTAL SCORE: ______ /7

Name ______________________________

Grammar: Adverbs

Choose the word or words that best complete each sentence.

1. Carla _____ ate her picnic lunch.
   - (A) fast
   - (B) most lazy
   - (C) more fastly
   - (D) lazily

2. She met me on the playground _____.
   - (F) strongly
   - (G) today
   - (H) under
   - (I) mostly

3. Joseph _____ read the directions before beginning the test.
   - (A) most anxious
   - (B) carefully
   - (C) yesterday
   - (D) knowledge

4. Students use computers _____ today than in the past.
   - (F) more often
   - (G) most often
   - (H) more oftener
   - (I) most oftener

TOTAL SCORE: _____ /4

Name ______________________________

Weekly Lesson Test

Lesson 28

Oral Reading Fluency

Samantha had felt extremely nervous during the last week of the school year. Samantha's mother had planned for her to go to summer camp. Samantha had never spent the night away from home without her mother, and none of her school friends was going to summer camp. Samantha complained to her mother that she wanted to stay home, but her mother just smiled and encouraged her to keep an open mind.

On the first day of camp, Samantha was afraid—she did not know anyone. However, she felt better after she met the camp counselor, Anita, who played games and sang songs with the campers. Before long, Samantha learned the other campers' names. The girls who stayed in her cabin came from all over the state where Samantha lived.

During her week at camp, Samantha made candles in her craft class, rode horses, and explored nature trails. At night Samantha and her friends sang songs around a campfire, and they enjoyed watching the stars.

When Samantha's mother came to pick her up, Samantha hugged her new friends and waved goodbye. As she fastened her seatbelt in the car, she asked if she could come back next summer. Her mother smiled, not at all surprised.

______ /WCPM

Name ____________________

Weekly Lesson Test
Lesson 29

Selection Comprehension

Choose the best answer for each question.

1. Why was John Muir called "Ice Chief"?
   Ⓐ He enjoyed walking in snow.
   Ⓑ He was an expert on glaciers.
   Ⓒ He survived a winter storm.
   Ⓓ He was in charge of the camp.

2. Why didn't Muir want Stickeen to follow him out of camp?
   Ⓕ He knew the dog was unfriendly.
   Ⓖ He thought the dog would run away.
   Ⓗ He believed the dog was unfit for the outdoors.
   Ⓘ He wanted to go with his crew rather than a dog.

3. Which action BEST shows that Muir has begun to care for Stickeen?
   Ⓐ He offers Stickeen some of his food.
   Ⓑ He tells Stickeen to go back to camp.
   Ⓒ He slips out without waking Stickeen.
   Ⓓ He leaves Stickeen to do as he wishes.

4. Why does the author compare Stickeen's eyes to "weather that could turn on you"?
   Ⓕ to show that Stickeen had unusual eyes
   Ⓖ to prove that Stickeen was a mean dog
   Ⓗ to show that John did not trust Stickeen
   Ⓘ to prove Hall was right about Stickeen

5. What is the main idea in "John Muir and Stickeen"?
   Ⓐ Dogs are good to have along when traveling.
   Ⓑ Exploring glaciers can be cold and dangerous work.
   Ⓒ It can be very hard to survive a bad storm in the wilderness.
   Ⓓ Humans and animals can form a friendship in difficult times.

Name ______________________________

Weekly Lesson Test
Lesson 29

6. How are John Muir and Stickeen ALIKE?
   Ⓕ Both are brave.
   Ⓖ Both love the ice.
   Ⓗ Both can swim well.
   Ⓘ Both have herded sheep.

7. Why does the author compare Stickeen to a cold and silent glacier?
   Ⓐ to explain why Stickeen is not wanted on the trip
   Ⓑ to show that Stickeen likes to be out on the ice
   Ⓒ to explain why Stickeen is shaking and shivering
   Ⓓ to show that Stickeen had not yet accepted John as a friend

8. How do you know that "John Muir and Stickeen" is historical fiction?
   Ⓕ It has acts that are divided into scenes.
   Ⓖ It gives facts and information about a topic.
   Ⓗ It has real people and events that really happened.
   Ⓘ It has humor and tells about impossible happenings.

Written Response

9. What lesson do you think Stickeen helped John Muir learn about animals? Use details from "John Muir and Stickeen" to explain your answer.

____

____

____

____

____

TOTAL SCORE: ______ /8 + ______ /2

Name ___________________________________

Weekly Lesson Test
Lesson 29

Focus Skill: Figurative Language

▶ **Read the passage. Then choose the best answer for each question.**

Tea Party with My Aunt

I remember the first time I drank tea as if it were yesterday. My aunt had invited me over because my mother had to attend a meeting. My aunt was as sly as a fox. She knew I would prefer a tea party to having a babysitter all afternoon. At my age, the suggestion that I needed a babysitter was a criminal offense.

My aunt set up our tea party in her backyard. She placed a lovely cloth over a large cardboard box. She used real china teacups she had found at a garage sale. This was no baby's tea party, but the real thing.

She served tiny sandwiches she had made. She said she had once seen similar food in a teahouse. The sandwiches were as small as the teabags. It seems that fancy teahouses serve food meant for dolls instead of real people!

We chatted quite a bit about school and family. Soon I noticed that my throat was a parched desert from all our talking. As I gulped the tea, a streak of fire poured down my throat. I had been expecting iced tea, not hot tea! Despite drinking the hot tea, the tea party was as special as Cinderella's ball. I was grinning like a jack o'lantern when my mother came to pick me up. It was clear that my aunt had pulled it off. After that, my mother no longer had a problem finding a babysitter for me. I had many more wonderful tea parties with my aunt. However, we drank iced tea at those parties!

Name ______________________________

1. In the first sentence, what does the phrase "as if it were yesterday" mean?
   Ⓐ The author remembers the event clearly.
   Ⓑ The event happened yesterday.
   Ⓒ The author remembers only part of the event.
   Ⓓ The event is a dim memory.

2. Which of the following is an example of a simile?
   Ⓕ My throat was a dry desert.
   Ⓖ This was no baby's tea party.
   Ⓗ My aunt was as sly as a fox.
   Ⓘ A streak of fire poured down my throat.

3. Which of the following is an example of hyperbole?
   Ⓐ She served tiny sandwiches she had made.
   Ⓑ She placed a lovely cloth over a large cardboard box.
   Ⓒ She used real china teacups that she had found at a garage sale.
   Ⓓ At my age, the suggestion that I needed a babysitter was a criminal offense.

4. What does the author mean when she says that her aunt had "pulled it off"?
   Ⓕ She had planned a Cinderella ball.
   Ⓖ She had learned how to be sly like a fox.
   Ⓗ She had successfully babysat all afternoon.
   Ⓘ She had planned a great tea party.

Name ______________________________

Weekly Lesson Test
Lesson 29

Robust Vocabulary

▶ **Choose the best word to complete each sentence.**

1. In order to see the volcano, we ______ a four-hour bus ride.

   Ⓐ cascaded
   Ⓑ embedded
   Ⓒ glistened
   Ⓓ endured

2. The ______ runner finished the race even though it was raining hard.

   Ⓕ determined
   Ⓖ scenic
   Ⓗ coddled
   Ⓘ dainty

3. He had taught for many years and was ______ to helping his students learn.

   Ⓐ coddled
   Ⓑ embedded
   Ⓒ submerged
   Ⓓ dedicated

4. The children took turns petting and feeding their ______ pet bunny special bunny treats.

   Ⓕ determined
   Ⓖ coddled
   Ⓗ pitiful
   Ⓘ colossal

Name ______________________________

Weekly Lesson Test
Lesson 29

5. The little doll wore a ______ lace dress with a matching bonnet.
   Ⓐ pitiful
   Ⓑ determined
   Ⓒ dainty
   Ⓓ behemoth

6. The fireworks show was ______ because it had so many different colors and patterns.
   Ⓕ pitiful
   Ⓖ dainty
   Ⓗ memorable
   Ⓘ coddled

7. After walking home in the rain, the poor dog looked ______.
   Ⓐ dainty
   Ⓑ pitiful
   Ⓒ memorable
   Ⓓ coddled

TOTAL SCORE: ______ /7

Name ______________________________

Weekly Lesson Test
Lesson 29

Grammar: Punctuation Review

Choose the best answer for each question.

1. Which of the following is the correct way to write the title of a book?

   Ⓐ *The World According to Humphrey*

   Ⓑ *The world according to Humphrey*

   Ⓒ The World According to Humphrey

   Ⓓ "The World According to Humphrey"

2. Which of the following sentences is properly punctuated?

   Ⓕ We ate peas carrots and barley.

   Ⓖ We ate peas carrots, and barley.

   Ⓗ We ate peas, carrots, and barley.

   Ⓘ We ate, peas, carrots, and barley.

3. Which of the following sentences is properly punctuated?

   Ⓐ The cook yelled, "Come and get it!"

   Ⓑ The cook yelled; "Come and get it!"

   Ⓒ The cook yelled Come and get it!

   Ⓓ "The cook yelled," Come and get it!

4. Which of the following sentences is properly punctuated?

   Ⓕ Well we might sing Yankee Doodle after the fireworks.

   Ⓖ Well, we might sing "Yankee" Doodle after the fireworks.

   Ⓗ Well we might sing *Yankee Doodle* after the fireworks.

   Ⓘ Well, we might sing "Yankee Doodle" after the fireworks.

TOTAL SCORE: ______ /4

Name ______________________________

Oral Reading Fluency

As a youth, Dr. Sylvia Earle moved with her family from New Jersey to Florida. She was completely amazed by the Gulf Coast and the animals living there. Since then Dr. Earle has worked to help others understand and care for sea life around the world. She has made films and studied in labs. She even started two companies that make underwater vehicles.

Dr. Earle once lived on the ocean floor for two weeks. She lived in a kind of hotel under the water. It had a kitchen, carpeted bedrooms, and hot showers. Naturally, it also had a lab for studying ocean life.

When she went outside of the hotel, Dr. Earle used a special machine that recycles a person's air. It works like the systems astronauts use on the moon. It can be used for up to twelve hours.

During her stay underwater, Dr. Earle studied the nearby coral reef. It was so interesting that she barely slept or ate during the entire two weeks. She saw things others had never seen before. She learned things that were not in books. "If I could, I would have been outside 24 hours a day," she later said.

______ /WCPM

Name ______________________________

Weekly
Lesson Test
Lesson 30

Selection Comprehension

Choose the best answer for each question.

1. The history of the *Atocha* is MOSTLY told by
   - Ⓐ Mel.
   - Ⓑ Kane.
   - Ⓒ Duncan.
   - Ⓓ Narrators 1 and 2.

2. Why did the author write "Discovering the *Atocha*"?
   - Ⓕ to tell how a crew found a lost ship
   - Ⓖ to explain an easy way to find treasure
   - Ⓗ to warn readers about diving for treasure
   - Ⓘ to persuade readers to hunt for sunken ships

3. Which of these is an OPINION from the selection?
   - Ⓐ The *Atocha* sank after being caught in a hurricane in 1622.
   - Ⓑ We've been at this twice a day for the past nine months.
   - Ⓒ Flying above the water is certainly easier than scuba diving.
   - Ⓓ There are 882 islands in the Keys!

4. Why does Mel want to fly above the Keys?
   - Ⓕ He is tired of being on the boat.
   - Ⓖ He believes that diving is useless.
   - Ⓗ He thinks the view will be beautiful.
   - Ⓘ He has an idea about a new place to explore.

5. Which would MOST help a reader understand the ideas in this selection?
   - Ⓐ using a metal detector at school
   - Ⓑ looking at pictures of diving gear
   - Ⓒ going to Florida for a family vacation
   - Ⓓ reading about another search for an old ship

Name ________________________________

Weekly Lesson Test
Lesson 30

6. Juan signals the divers to return to the surface because he
   Ⓕ thinks they are in danger.
   Ⓖ believes his metal detector is broken.
   Ⓗ wants to call Mel on the two-way radio.
   Ⓘ is sure they have been underwater too long.

7. What is the MAIN reason Mel says ". . . the work is just beginning"?
   Ⓐ They must search to find the rest of the cannon.
   Ⓑ The remains of the ship must be recovered and studied.
   Ⓒ They will have to spend many years finding another ship.
   Ⓓ It is hard to bring the ship up from the bottom of the ocean.

8. Which action BEST shows that Mel Fisher is a determined person?
   Ⓕ He called his helpers the "Golden Crew."
   Ⓖ He read a book about hunting for treasure.
   Ⓗ He kept searching for more than fifteen years.
   Ⓘ He invented a machine to help clear the water.

Written Response

9. Would you like to search for treasure in the ocean like Mel Fisher? Explain why you would or would not enjoy searching for treasure. Use details from "Discovering the *Atocha*" to support your answer.

____

____

____

____

TOTAL SCORE: ______ /8 + ______ /2

Name ______________________________

Weekly Lesson Test
Lesson 30

Robust Vocabulary

▶ **Choose the word that best completes each sentence.**

1. During the test, I made sure to _____ each answer for mistakes.
   Ⓐ scrutinize
   Ⓑ estimate
   Ⓒ descend
   Ⓓ discern

2. People in the _____ of the airport often hear airplanes.
   Ⓕ sentry
   Ⓖ obstacle
   Ⓗ illusion
   Ⓘ vicinity

3. She _____ tried to finish the report before it was due.
   Ⓐ cordially
   Ⓑ frantically
   Ⓒ abruptly
   Ⓓ expectantly

4. The fog rolled in and we could not _____ where the road was.
   Ⓕ endure
   Ⓖ descend
   Ⓗ discern
   Ⓘ dedicate

5. The painting proudly showed the queen's _____ ancestors.
   Ⓐ dubious
   Ⓑ submerged
   Ⓒ distinguished
   Ⓓ complicated

Name ______________________________

Weekly Lesson Test

Lesson 30

6. My friend made a _____ claim that his father's basketball team had never lost a game.

Ⓕ coddled

Ⓖ dainty

Ⓗ dubious

Ⓘ distinguished

7. You have to _____ a steep stairway to the basement.

Ⓐ descend

Ⓑ verify

Ⓒ estimate

Ⓓ scrutinize

8. The roller coaster ride ended _____ with a sudden stop.

Ⓕ frantically

Ⓖ cordially

Ⓗ abruptly

Ⓘ forlornly

9. The man had papers to _____ that his dog was a champion.

Ⓐ discern

Ⓑ descend

Ⓒ scrutinize

Ⓓ verify

10. Without a scale, we had to _____ the fish's weight.

Ⓕ erode

Ⓖ estimate

Ⓗ endure

Ⓘ descend

TOTAL SCORE: _____ /10